ARM 56 Course Guide

Risk Financing
5th Edition

American Institute for Chartered Property Casualty Underwriters/Insurance Institute of America

720 Providence Road • Suite 100 • Malvern, PA 19355-3433

© 2008

American Institute for Chartered Property Casualty Underwriters/Insurance Institute of America

All rights reserved. This book or any part thereof may not be reproduced without the written permission of the copyright holder.

Unless otherwise apparent, examples used in AICPCU/IIA materials related to this course are based on hypothetical situations and are for educational purposes only. The characters, persons, products, services, and organizations described in these examples are fictional. Any similarity or resemblance to any other character, person, product, services, or organization is merely coincidental. AICPCU/IIA is not responsible for such coincidental or accidental resemblances.

This material may contain Internet Web site links external to AICPCU/IIA. AICPCU/IIA neither approves nor endorses any information, products, or services to which any external Web sites refer. Nor does AICPCU/IIA control these Web sites' content or the procedures for Web site content development.

AICPCU/IIA specifically disclaims any implied warranties of merchantability or fitness for a particular purpose. No warranty may be created or extended by sales representatives or written sales materials.

AICPCU/IIA materials related to this course are provided with the understanding that AICPCU/IIA is not engaged in rendering legal, accounting, or other professional service. Nor is AICPCU/IIA explicitly or implicitly stating that any of the processes, procedures, or policies described in the materials are the only appropriate ones to use. The advice and strategies contained herein may not be suitable for every situation.

Fifth Edition • Third Printing • February 2010

ISBN 978-0-89463-372-0

Contents

Study Materials iii
Student Resources iv
Using This Course Guide iv
ARM Advisory Committee vi

Assignments
1. Understanding Risk Financing 1.1
2. Insurance as a Risk Financing Technique 2.1
3. Insurance Plan Design 3.1
4. Forecasting Accidental Losses and Risk Financing Needs 4.1
5. Self-Insurance Plans 5.1
6. Retrospective Rating Plans 6.1
7. Reinsurance and Its Importance to a Risk Financing Program 7.1
8. Captive Insurance Plans 8.1
9. Finite and Integrated Risk Insurance Plans 9.1
10. Capital Market Risk Financing Plans 10.1
11. Noninsurance Contractual Transfer of Risk 11.1
12. Purchasing Insurance and Other Risk Financing Services 12.1
13. Allocating Risk Management Costs 13.1
Exam Information 1

Study Materials Available for ARM 56

Richard G. Berthelsen, Michael W. Elliott, Connor M. Harrison, *Risk Financing*, 4th ed., 2006, AICPCU/IIA.

ARM 56 *Course Guide*, 5th ed., 2008, AICPCU/IIA (includes access code for SMART Online Practice Exams).

ARM 56 SMART Study Aids—Review Notes and Flash Cards, 2nd ed.

Student Resources

Catalog A complete listing of our offerings can be found in *Succeed*, the Institutes' professional development catalog, including information about:

- Current programs and courses
- Current textbooks, course guides, and SMART Study Aids
- Program completion requirements
- Exam registration

To obtain a copy of the catalog, visit our Web site at www.aicpcu.org or contact Customer Service at (800) 644-2101.

How to Prepare for Institute Exams This free handbook is designed to help you by:

- Giving you ideas on how to use textbooks and course guides as effective learning tools
- Providing steps for answering exam questions effectively
- Recommending exam-day strategies

The handbook is printable from the Student Services Center on the Institutes' Web site at www.aicpcu.org, or available by calling Customer Service at (800) 644-2101.

Educational Counseling Services To ensure that you take courses matching both your needs and your skills, you can obtain free counseling from the Institutes by:

- E-mailing your questions to advising@cpcuiia.org
- Calling an Institutes' counselor directly at (610) 644-2100, ext. 7601
- Obtaining and completing a self-inventory form, available on our Web site at www.aicpcu.org or by contacting Customer Service at (800) 644-2101

Exam Registration Information As you proceed with your studies, be sure to arrange for your exam.

- Visit our Web site at www.aicpcu.org/forms to access and print the Registration Booklet, which contains information and forms needed to register for your exam.
- Plan to register with the Institutes well in advance of your exam.

How to Contact the Institutes For more information on any of these publications and services:

- Visit our Web site at www.aicpcu.org
- Call us at (800) 644-2101 or (610) 644-2100 outside the U.S.
- E-mail us at customerservice@cpcuiia.org
- Fax us at (610) 640-9576
- Write to us at AICPCU/IIA, Customer Service, 720 Providence Road, Suite 100, Malvern, PA 19355-3433

Using This Course Guide

This course guide will help you learn the course content and prepare for the exam.

Each assignment in this course guide typically includes the following components:

Educational Objectives These are the most important study tools in the course guide. Because all of the questions on the exam are based on the Educational Objectives, the best way to study for the exam is to focus on these objectives.

Each Educational Objective typically begins with one of the following action words, which indicate the level of understanding required for the exam:

Analyze—Determine the nature and the relationship of the parts.

Apply—Put to use for a practical purpose.

Associate—Bring together into relationship.

Calculate—Determine numeric values by mathematical process.

Classify—Arrange or organize according to class or category.

Compare—Show similarities and differences.

Contrast—Show only differences.

Define—Give a clear, concise meaning.

Describe—Represent or give an account.

Determine—Settle or decide.

Evaluate—Determine the value or merit.

Explain—Relate the importance or application.

Identify or list—Name or make a list.

Illustrate—Give an example.

Justify—Show to be right or reasonable.

Paraphrase—Restate in your own words.

Summarize—Concisely state the main points.

Required Reading The items listed in this section indicate the study materials (the textbook chapter(s), course guide readings, or other assigned materials) that correspond to the assignment.

Outline The outline lists the topics in the assignment. Read the outline before the required reading to become familiar with the assignment content and the relationships of topics.

Key Words and Phrases These words and phrases are fundamental to understanding the assignment and have a common meaning for those working in insurance. After completing the required reading, test your understanding of the assignment's Key Words and Phrases by writing their definitions.

Review Questions The review questions test your understanding of what you have read. Review the Educational Objectives and required reading, then answer the questions to the best of your ability. When you are finished, check the answers at the end of the assignment to evaluate your comprehension.

Application Questions These questions continue to test your knowledge of the required reading by applying what you've studied to "hypothetical" real-life situations. Again, check the suggested answers at the end of the assignment to review your progress.

Sample Exam Your course guide includes either a sample exam (located at the back) or a code for accessing SMART Online Practice Exams (which appears on the inside back cover). Use this supplemental exam material to become familiar with the test format and to practice answering exam questions.

For courses that offer SMART Online Practice Exams, you can both download and print a sample credentialing exam and take full practice exams using the same software you will use when you take your credentialing exam. SMART Online Practice Exams are as close as you can get to experiencing an actual exam before taking one.

More Study Aids

The Institutes also produce supplemental study tools, called SMART Study Aids, for many of our courses. When SMART Study Aids are available for a course, they are listed on both page iii of this course guide and on the first page of each assignment. SMART Study Aids include Review Notes and Flash Cards and are excellent tools to help you learn and retain the information in each assignment.

ARM Advisory Committee

Bryan W. Barger, CPCU, ARM, ALCM
Marsh USA, Inc.

Karen L. Butcher, ARM
Aon Risk Services, Inc., of Ohio

Dr. Richard B. Corbett, CLU, CPCU, ARM
Florida State University

Donald E. Dresback, CPCU, ARM, AAI
The Beacon Group, Inc.

Mary Eisenhart, CPCU, ARM, ARe
Agency Management Resource Group

Elise M. Farnham, ARM, CPCU, CPIW
Illumine Consulting

Edward S. Katersky, ARM, CPCU, CSP
BJ's Wholesale Club, Inc.

Melissa Olsen Leuck, ARM
TAP Pharmaceutical Products, Inc.

Bill Mason, CPCU, ARM-P
Public Risk Management Association

Ludmilla Pieczatkowska, CPCU
William Gallagher Associates Insurance Brokers, Inc.

Jim Swanson, CRM, RF, FIIC
Government of Manitoba

Tom Worischeck, CSP, ARM
Kimmins Contracting Corp.

Direct Your Learning

Understanding Risk Financing

Educational Objectives

After learning the content of this assignment, you should be able to:

1. Describe risk financing and its importance to organizations.
2. Describe the following risk financing goals:
   - Paying for losses
   - Maintaining an appropriate level of liquidity
   - Managing uncertainty of loss outcomes
   - Managing the cost of risk
   - Complying with legal requirements
3. Explain how loss characteristics affect risk financing technique selection.
4. Explain how enterprise risk management provides a holistic approach to risk financing.
5. Define or describe each of the Key Words and Phrases for this assignment.

Study Materials

Required Reading:
- Risk Financing
  - Chapter 1

Study Aids:
- SMART Online Practice Exam
- SMART Study Aids
  - Review Notes and Flash Cards—Assignment 1

Outline

▶ **Risk Financing and Its Importance**
  A. Transfer
  B. Retention

▶ **Risk Financing Goals**
  A. Paying for Losses
  B. Maintaining an Appropriate Level of Liquidity
  C. Managing Uncertainty Resulting From Loss Outcomes
  D. Managing the Cost of Risk
    1. Administrative Expenses
    2. Risk Control Expenses
    3. Retained Losses
    4. Transfer Costs
  E. Complying With Legal Requirements

▶ **Risk Financing Technique Selection**

▶ **Enterprise Risk Management: A Holistic Approach to Risk Financing**

▶ **Summary**

Don't spend time on material you have already mastered. The SMART Review Notes are organized by the Educational Objectives found in each course guide assignment to help you track your study.

For each assignment, you should define or describe each of the Key Words and Phrases and answer each of the Review and Application Questions.

> ## Educational Objective 1
> Describe risk financing and its importance to organizations.

Key Words and Phrases

Risk financing (p. 1.4)

Insurance (p. 1.4)

Noninsurance risk transfer (p. 1.5)

Hold-harmless agreement (p. 1.5)

Hedging (p. 1.5)

Futures contract (p. 1.5)

Retention (p. 1.5)

Pre-loss funding (p. 1.6)

Current-loss funding (p. 1.6)

Post-loss funding (p. 1.6)

Review Questions

1-1. Describe the two categories of risk financing techniques used by organizations to generate funds to pay for losses or offset variability in cash flows. (p. 1.4)

1-2. Describe how the following types of noninsurance risk transfers enable an organization to fund financial consequences of a loss: (p. 1.5)

    a. Hold-harmless agreement

    b. Hedging

1-3. Describe the following types of retention that an organization may use to generate funds to pay for losses: (p 1.6)

   a. Planned retention

   b. Unplanned retention

   c. Complete retention

   d. Partial retention

   e. Funded retention

   f. Unfunded retention

1-4. Describe the advantages and disadvantages of using the following methods to pay for retained losses: (pp. 1.6–1.7)

   a. Pre-loss funding

   b. Current-loss funding

   c. Post-loss funding

Application Question

1-5. Sports Gear Manufacturer decided five years ago to pay for its products liability losses out of its earnings. Products liability losses are now significantly diminishing earnings. How may Sports Gear Manufacturer's risk management professional more economically fund the following types of losses?

   a. Existing losses

   b. Future losses

Educational Objective 2

Describe the following risk financing goals:
- Paying for losses
- Maintaining an appropriate level of liquidity
- Managing uncertainty of loss outcomes
- Managing the cost of risk
- Complying with legal requirements

Review Questions

2-1. Identify common risk financing goals an organization may pursue. (p. 1.8)

2-2. Describe the relationship between an organization's loss retention level and its need for liquidity. (p. 1.8)

2-3 Identify the factors that may affect an organization's maximum uncertainty level. (p. 1.9)

2-4. Describe the difference between hazard risk and business risk. (p. 1.9)

2-5. Describe the expenses that form part of the cost of risk. (p. 1.9)

Application Question

2-6. Fast Food Restaurant's risk management professional has proposed a comprehensive retention program to handle its hazard risk. According to its risk management professional, the retention program will result in long-term savings; however, the organization can expect to endure higher-than-expected losses in some years. How will this retention program affect the organization's current market value?

Educational Objective 3
Explain how loss characteristics affect risk financing technique selection.

Review Questions

3-1. Identify the loss characteristics used by risk management professionals when selecting risk financing techniques. (pp. 1.11–1.12)

3-2. Describe an organization's probable decision regarding retention of losses with the following frequency-severity characteristics: (p. 1.12)

   a. Low severity and low frequency

   b. High severity and low frequency

   c. Low severity and high frequency

   d. Medium severity and medium frequency

3-3. Identify the loss characteristics for which the following risk financing plans are appropriate: (p. 1.12)

   a. Retention plans

   b. Transfer plans

Application Question

3-4. For each of the following situations, select the most appropriate risk financing plan (retention, transfer, or hybrid) for the given organization based on the given loss exposure's relative frequency and severity:

   a. Local Package Delivery experiences frequent physical damage losses to its trucks.

   b. National Farm Products wants to protect its poultry operations from the possible financial consequences of an avian flu outbreak.

c. Construction Contractor recognizes that worker injuries are an unfortunate consequence of doing business.

Educational Objective 4
Explain how enterprise risk management provides a holistic approach to risk financing.

Key Words and Phrases
Enterprise risk management (ERM) (p. 1.13)

Business risk (p. 1.13)

Review Questions

4-1. Explain why an organization may use enterprise risk management to manage its business risks. (p. 1.13)

4-2. Identify the categories of risk that enterprise risk management is commonly used to manage. (p. 1.13)

4-3. Describe the differences between enterprise risk management and traditional risk management. (p. 1.14)

Application Question

4-4. National Bank is a leader in the home mortgage business. Consequently, its operations are significantly affected by changes in interest rates. National Bank is considering the benefits of enterprise risk management. Identify the risks that it may be able to address with enterprise risk management.

Answers to Assignment 1 Questions

NOTE: These answers are provided to give students a basic understanding of acceptable types of responses. They often are not the only valid answers and are not intended to provide an exhaustive response to the questions.

Educational Objective 1

1-1. The following two categories of risk financing techniques may be used by organizations to generate funds to pay for losses or offset variability in cash flows:

(1) Transfer—Organization shifts financial consequences of loss to another party through insurance and noninsurance techniques.

(2) Retention—Organization absorbs loss by generating funds within the organization to pay for the loss.

1-2. An organization may use the following types of noninsurance risk transfer to fund financial consequences of a loss:

a. Hold-harmless agreement—Assigns responsibility for a loss arising out of a particular relationship or activity. One party (the indemnitor) agrees to assume the liability of a second party (the indemnitee).

b. Hedging—Offsets loss exposures to which one is naturally, voluntarily, or inevitably exposed. One asset is held to offset the risk associated with another asset.

1-3. An organization may use the following types of retention to generate funds to pay for losses:

a. Planned retention—a deliberate assumption of a loss exposure (and any consequential losses) that has been identified and analyzed

b. Unplanned retention—inadvertent assumption of a loss exposure (and any consequential losses) that has not been identified or accurately analyzed

c. Complete retention—assumption of the full cost of any loss that is retained by the organization

d. Partial retention—assumption of a portion of the cost of a loss by the organization and the transfer of the remaining portion

e. Funded retention—pre-loss arrangement to ensure that funding is available after a loss to pay for losses that occur

f. Unfunded retention—lack of advance funding for losses that occur

1-4. The advantages and disadvantages of using the given methods to pay for retained losses are as follows:

a. Pre-loss funding
- Advantage—The money needed to fund losses can be saved over several budget periods.
- Disadvantage—Ties up money that could otherwise be used by the organization

b. Current-loss funding
- Advantage—Does not tie up funds before they are needed.
- Disadvantage—There may not be enough money in the current budget to cover the given loss and satisfy other cash flow needs.

c. Post-loss funding
- Advantages—(1) Cost of retained losses can be paid over several years and (2) only the amount needed to pay for retained losses is used.
- Disadvantage—(1) The organization must pay interest on the borrowed funds, (2) the loss event that produces the need to borrow may also reduce the organization's creditworthiness, and (3) guaranteeing post-loss credit may reduce the organization's capacity to borrow pre-loss funds for business operations.

1-5. a. Sports Gear Manufacturer's risk management professional should consider sources of funds other than earnings, such as borrowing or some other method of raising capital, because earnings could prove to be insufficient to pay for products liability losses. Sports Gear Manufacturer should switch from current-loss funding to post-loss funding arrangements.

b. Sports Gear Manufacturer's risk management professional should consider using pre-loss funding arrangements because of the significance of these losses. A pre-loss funding arrangement would allow Sports Gear Manufacturer to fund losses after several budget periods.

Educational Objective 2

2-1. Common risk financing goals an organization may pursue include the following:
- Paying for losses
- Maintaining an appropriate level of liquidity
- Managing uncertainty of loss outcomes
- Managing the cost of risk
- Complying with legal requirements

2-2. The relationship between an organization's loss retention level and its need for liquidity is as follows:

The higher an organization's retention, the greater the need for liquidity. Organizations that retain losses and have extensive loss variability and, consequently, greater uncertainty also need substantial liquidity.

2-3. An organization's maximum uncertainty level may be affected by its size, its financial strength, and its level of tolerance.

2-4. Hazard risk is the possibility of accidental loss arising from property, liability, personnel, and net income loss exposures. Business risk presents the possibility of loss and also of gain.

2-5. The expenses that form the cost of risk include the following:
- Administrative expenses—includes an organization's cost of internal administration and its cost of purchased services
- Risk control expenses—includes expenses incurred to prevent losses or reduce the severity of losses that do occur
- Retained losses—includes expenses that are the major component of an organization's cost of risk
- Transfer costs—includes amounts an organization pays to outside organizations to transfer its cost of risk

2-6. The higher the risk associated with future cash flows, the greater the discount rate. The greater the discount rate, the lower the present value of an organization's cash flow and the lower the market value that investors assign the organization. While Fast Food Restaurant may enjoy long-term savings through a retention program, investors may not reward that proposal because the increased variability in the organization's cash flow reduces the organization's market value. Consequently, the risk management professional must recognize the effect of risk management decisions on the value of the organization.

Educational Objective 3

3-1. Risk management professionals use the following loss characteristics when selecting risk financing techniques:
- Loss frequency—the number of losses that occur within a specified period
- Loss severity—the amount of a loss, typically measured in dollars, for a loss that has occurred

3-2. The probable decisions regarding retention of losses with the following frequency-severity characteristics include the following:
   a. Low-severity and low-frequency losses—Losses are predictable and are usually of little financial consequence. These types of losses would likely be retained by an organization.
   b. High-severity and low-frequency losses—Cost of these losses is unpredictable and they present a high risk to organizations. These types of losses would likely be transferred before they occur.
   c. Low-severity and high-frequency losses—Losses are predictable. These types of losses would likely be retained by an organization.
   d. Medium-severity and medium-frequency losses—Organizations may retain or transfer these losses, depending on their tolerance for risk and the cost of risk transfer.

3-3. The loss characteristics for which the following risk financing plans are appropriate include:
   a. Retention plans—Low-severity losses
   b. Transfer plans—High-severity losses

3-4. a. Because Local Package Delivery has frequent, relatively small losses, it should consider a risk financing plan that uses retention. A hybrid plan also should be considered if its accumulated losses are significant.
   b. Because National Farm Products has a potentially catastrophic exposure to an avian flu outbreak, it should consider risk transfer to finance risk. The magnitude of this exposure and the likelihood that some aspects of this loss exposure are uninsurable may induce it to consider a hybrid plan.
   c. Because workers' compensation losses occur with some regularity and can be significant, Construction Contractor may consider transfer, retention, and hybrid plans. The "best" plan for it depends on how accurately it can predict its losses.

Educational Objective 4

4-1. An organization may decide to manage business risks by using the enterprise risk management approach to risk financing to maximize shareholders value.

4-2. Enterprise risk management manages the following categories of risk:

- Strategic risks—uncertainties associated with an organization's overall long-term goals and management
- Operational risks—uncertainties associated with an organization's operations
- Financial risks—uncertainties associated with an organization's financial activities
- Hazard risks—uncertainties associated with an organization's reduction in value resulting from the effects of accidental losses

4-3. Enterprise risk management and traditional risk management differ in scope. Traditional risk management deals only with hazard risk, while enterprise risk management deals with hazard and business risk.

4-4. Interest rate fluctuation is National Bank's most significant risk. Because National Bank is a financial intermediary, interest rate fluctuation is not only a financial risk, but also an operational risk. To the extent that interest rate fluctuation affects National Bank's overall, long-term goals, it is a strategic risk. National Bank may be able to use ERM to address these risks.

Direct Your Learning

Insurance as a Risk Financing Technique

Educational Objectives

After learning the content of this assignment, you should be able to:

1. Describe the purpose and operation of insurance, including:
   - Risk reduction through pooling
   - Services provided by insurers
2. Describe the characteristics of an ideally insurable loss exposure.
3. Describe the types of insurance that address specific loss exposures.
4. Describe the advantages and disadvantages of insurance.
5. Define or describe each of the Key Words and Phrases for this assignment.

Study Materials

Required Reading:
- Risk Financing
  - Chapter 2

Study Aids:
- SMART Online Practice Exam
- SMART Study Aids
  - Review Notes and Flash Cards—Assignment 2

Outline

- **Purpose and Operation of Insurance**
    - A. Pooling
        1. How Pooling Reduces Risk
        2. How the Law of Large Numbers Explains Pooling
        3. How Positively Correlated Losses Affect a Pool
        4. How Insurance Differs From Pooling
    - B. Insurer-Provided Risk Management Services
        1. Risk Control Services
        2. Claim and Legal Services
- **Characteristics of an Ideally Insurable Loss Exposure**
    - A. Pure Risk
    - B. Fortuitous Losses
    - C. Definite and Measurable
    - D. Homogenous
    - E. Independent and Not Catastrophic
    - F. Affordable
- **Types of Insurance That Address Specific Loss Exposures**
    - A. Property Insurance
    - B. Business Income Insurance
    - C. General Liability Insurance
    - D. Auto Insurance
    - E. Workers' Compensation and Employers' Liability Insurance
    - F. Flood Insurance
    - G. Directors and Officers Liability Insurance
    - H. Employment Practices Liability Insurance
    - I. Professional Liability Insurance
    - J. Environmental Insurance
    - K. Aircraft Insurance
    - L. Umbrella Liability Insurance
    - M. Surety Bonds
    - N. Ocean Marine Insurance
    - O. Inland Marine Insurance
    - P. Crime Insurance
    - Q. Equipment Breakdown Insurance
    - R. Businessowners Insurance
    - S. Difference in Conditions Insurance
- **Advantages and Disadvantages of Insurance**
    - A. Advantages of Insurance as a Risk Financing Technique
    - B. Disadvantages of Insurance as a Risk Financing Technique
- **Summary**

Reduce the number of Key Words and Phrases that you must review. SMART Flash Cards contain the Key Words and Phrases and their definitions, allowing you to set aside those cards that you have mastered.

For each assignment, you should define or describe each of the Key Words and Phrases and answer each of the Review and Application Questions.

Educational Objective 1

Describe the purpose and operation of insurance, including:

- Risk reduction through pooling
- Services provided by insurers

Key Words and Phrases

Pool (p. 2.4)

Law of large numbers (p. 2.9)

Risk charge (p. 2.11)

Counterparty risk (p. 2.11)

Review Questions

1-1. Identify the circumstances in which pooling reduces risk. (p. 2.4)

1-2. Describe the effect of pooling on an organization's expected accidental losses. (pp. 2.6–2.7)

1-3. Describe the typical distribution of positively correlated losses. (p. 2.9)

1-4. Identify two ways that insurance and pooling differ. (pp. 2.10–2.11)

1-5. Describe the services, in addition to risk transfer, that are often provided by insurers. (pp. 2.11–2.12)

Application Question

1-6. The Radley Bus Company is a publicly held corporation providing school bus transportation to public and private schools in Midland County. Radley owns 200 school buses, located in three different cities within the county. Its major competitors are two larger bus companies that operate in the same general area.

    a. Give one example in each of the following categories of a loss exposure Radley faces:

       (1) Correlated

       (2) Uncorrelated

    b. Suppose Radley were to enter into a formal arrangement with the Green Bus Company, a similar company that operates in another state, to pool the losses suffered by both companies. How would this affect Radley's risks with respect to each of the loss exposures previously identified? Explain.

    c. Suppose, instead, Radley were to participate in a formal pool with fifteen other school bus companies. How, if at all, would this affect Radley's risks with respect to each of the previously identified loss exposures? Explain.

Educational Objective 2
Describe the characteristics of an ideally insurable loss exposure.

Review Questions

2-1. List the six characteristics of an ideally insurable loss exposure. (p. 2.13)

2-2. Describe characteristics and insurability of each of the following: (p. 2.13)
   a. Pure risk

   b. Speculative risk

2-3. Identify ways in which an insurer may minimize the financial effect of potential catastrophic losses. (p. 2.15)

Application Question

2-4. Disasters involving hurricanes and flooding have raised questions about why a hurricane is considered an insurable cause of loss, while a flood is not. Use each of the six characteristics of an ideally insurable loss exposure to evaluate the commercial insurability of loss caused by flood.

Educational Objective 3
Describe the types of insurance that address specific loss exposures.

Key Word or Phrase
Manuscript policy (p. 2.16)

Review Questions

3-1 Describe the coverage forms that may be used to insure commercial property. (p. 2.17)

3-2. Explain why risk management professionals are interested in covered causes of loss and exclusions. (pp. 2.16, 2.18)

3-3. Describe two ISO policy forms used for business income insurance. (p. 2.20)

3-4. Describe two versions of the ISO Commercial General Liability (CGL) Coverage Form used to provide CGL insurance. (pp. 2.20–2.21)

3-5. Describe the coverage provided by the following ISO commercial auto coverage forms. (pp. 2.21–2.22)

    a. Business Auto Coverage Form

    b. Garage Coverage Form

    c. Truckers Coverage Form

3-6. Identify the portions of the workers' compensation and employers' liability policy developed by NCCI. (p. 2.22)

3-7. Identify the main policy form used by NFIP to provide flood insurance on commercial buildings and contents. (p. 2.22)

3-8. Describe the two insuring agreements traditionally contained in directors and officers (D&O) liability policies. (p. 2.23)

3-9. Identify the three main purposes of a commercial umbrella liability policy. (p. 2.24)

3-10. Describe the roles of the following parties involved in a surety bond: (p. 2.25)
   a. Obligee

b. Principal

c. Surety

3-11. Describe the following categories of surety bonds: (p. 2.25)
a. Contract bonds

b. License and permit bonds

c. Court bonds

d. Miscellaneous bonds

3-12. Describe the attributes of nonfiled commercial inland marine insurance. (p. 2.26)

3-13. Explain how crime insurance complements commercial property insurance. (p. 2.26)

3-14. Identify what some organizations consider to be the most valuable aspect of equipment breakdown insurance. (p. 2.27)

3-15. Describe the purpose for which difference in conditions insurance is usually purchased. (p. 2.28)

Application Question

3-16. Shop and Gas is a combination convenience store and gasoline station. Identify four types of commercial insurance that Shop and Gas should consider purchasing.

Educational Objective 4
Describe the advantages and disadvantages of insurance.

Key Word or Phrase
Underwriting cycle (p. 2.32)

Review Questions

4-1. Identify the advantages and disadvantages of using insurance as a risk financing technique. (pp. 2.29, 2.31)

4-2. Describe the value of the following insurance services commonly provided to policyholders: (pp. 2.29–2.30)
   a. Claim handling

   b. Risk control

4-3. Describe the trends in insurance pricing and availability indicated by the following extremes of underwriting cycles: (p. 2.32)

a. Soft market

b. Hard market

Application Question

4-4. Local Municipality owns a significant number of insured properties. Its risk management professional has been asked to investigate switching from insurance to a risk financing program that relies primarily on risk retention.

a. Identify two advantages of insurance that may be important to Local Municipality.

b. Identify two disadvantages of insurance that may be important to Local Municipality.

Answers to Assignment 2 Questions

NOTE: These answers are provided to give students a basic understanding of acceptable types of responses. They often are not the only valid answers and are not intended to provide an exhaustive response to the questions.

Educational Objective 1

1-1. Pooling reduces risk when the pooled losses are independent (or uncorrelated). Losses are independent if they are not subject to a common cause of loss.

1-2. Pooling does not change accident frequency or severity, but does reduce the distribution of losses facing the organization and reduces the probability of extreme outcomes.

1-3. Losses that are positively correlated result in a distribution of losses with greater variability (higher standard deviation). Consequently, losses are less predictable.

1-4. Two ways in which insurance and pooling differ are (1) that insurance transfers risk from the insured to the insurer in exchange for premiums and (2) the insurer has additional financial resources from which it can fund losses.

1-5. In addition to risk transfer, insurer services often include the following:
- Risk control services—Insurers develop expertise in assessing and controlling risk and provide assistance both in identifying loss exposures and in recommending ways to control the associated risk of loss.
- Claim and legal services—Insurers develop expertise in settling claims, administering claim payments, and preventing fraud; managing medical and disability claims; systems to report, track, and pay for claims; and a network of legal resources.

1-6. a. (1) Correlated loss exposure—Any loss exposure that would affect all of the buses simultaneously would constitute a correlated loss exposure. For example, a design defect may require that all of Radley's buses be repaired.

   (2) Uncorrelated loss exposure—Any loss exposure that would not affect all of the buses simultaneously would constitute an uncorrelated loss exposure. For example, a serious traffic accident would cause physical damage to a single bus.

   b. (1) Correlated loss exposure—Assuming both Radley's and Green's buses included the same defective buses (correlated loss), the risks would be unchanged. If losses are not correlated, some risk could be reduced through pooling, though not as much if the losses were correlated.

   (2) Uncorrelated loss exposure—Although the number of serious accidents to which Radley would contribute would increase, the overall cost of these incidents would become more predictable, reducing Radley's risk.

   c. A pool with fifteen other school bus companies would further reduce Radley's risk involving uncorrelated loss exposures.

Educational Objective 2

2-1. The six ideal characteristics of an ideally insurable loss exposure are as follows:
   (1) Pure risk—involves pure, not speculative risk
   (2) Fortuitous losses—subject to fortuitous loss from the insured organization's standpoint
   (3) Definite and measurable—subject to losses that are definite in time, cause, and location
   (4) Homogenous—one of a large number of similar exposure units
   (5) Independent and not catastrophic—not subject to a loss that would simultaneously affect many other similar loss exposures; loss would not be catastrophic
   (6) Affordable—premiums are economically feasible

2-2. a. Pure risk is a chance of loss or no loss, but no chance of gain. The pure risk associated with a loss exposure is generally insurable.
   b. Speculative risk is a chance of loss, no loss, or gain. Some speculative risks are subject to risk financing techniques but insurance is not a risk financing technique applied to speculative risks.

2-3. An insurer might minimize the financial effect of potential catastrophic losses by:
   - Limiting the accumulated value of insured properties in a particular area
   - Purchasing reinsurance
   - Product diversity

2-4. Whether flood is a commercially insurable loss exposure should be considered in the context of the following six characteristics:
   (1) Pure risk—Flood involves pure risk; that is, there is no means to benefit from the occurrence of a flood.
   (2) Fortuitous losses—Flooding is often fortuitous, such as when rain causes a river to overflow its banks. However, flooding may be caused when a dam fails, which may not be accidental from the insured's perspective. Certain areas are prone to flooding, while others definitely are not.
   (3) Definite and measurable—Flooding is an event that is obvious when it occurs.
   (4) Homogenous—Property that is subject to damage by flooding is relatively homogenous or can be made more so through a classification scheme.
   (5) Independent and not catastrophic—Flooding does cause catastrophic loss. This is the primary reason that property exposed to flood is considered to be uninsurable.
   (6) Affordable—Because flood zones, or areas prone to flooding, are easily recognizable, unsubsidized property pricing for flood is usually not affordable.

Insurers have not made a market for flood insurance because it would involve a relatively significant subsidy from insured organizations that have little or no flood exposure.

Educational Objective 3

3-1. Commercial property insurance can be provided under several coverage forms, including the Building and Personal Property Coverage Form, and a businessowners form.

3-2. Risk management professionals need to understand the coverage provided by insurance. They are interested in covered causes of loss and exclusions because exclusions can create coverage gaps.

3-3. The following two ISO policy forms provide business income coverage:
   (1) Business Income (and Extra Expense) Coverage Form—covers both business income loss and extra expense losses
   (2) Business Income (without Extra Expense) Coverage Form—covers business income loss but covers extra expenses only to the extent that they reduce the business income loss

3-4. The following two versions of the ISO Commercial General Liability Coverage Form are used to provide CGL insurance:
   (1) Occurrence coverage form—covers bodily injury or property damage that occurs during the policy period, regardless of when claim is actually made against the insured organization
   (2) Claims-made coverage form—covers bodily injury or property damage that occurs after the retroactive date stated in the policy, but only if claim for the injury or damage is first made at some time during the policy period

3-5. The following coverages are provided using the corresponding ISO commercial auto coverage forms:
   a. Business Auto Coverage Form—designed to meet the auto insurance needs of most types of organizations
   b. Garage Coverage Form—designed to meet the special needs of automobile dealers and to provide garagekeepers coverage
   c. Truckers Coverage Form—designed to insure auto liability and physical damage loss exposures of individuals or organizations in the business of transporting the property of others

3-6. The workers' compensation and employers' liability policy developed by NCCI consists of a workers' compensation portion that covers the insured's obligations under relevant workers' compensation laws and a portion that covers the insured for common-law suits that arise out of employee injury or disease.

3-7. NFIP uses the Standard Flood Insurance Policy to provide flood insurance on commercial buildings and contents.

3-8. Directors and officers (D&O) liability policies traditionally contain the following insuring agreements:
   - Covers directors and officers of the insured corporation for their personal liability as directors and officers that results from a "wrongful act"
   - Covers the sums that the insured is required or permitted by law to pay to the directors and officers as indemnification

3-9. The following are the three main purposes of a commercial umbrella liability policy:
   (1) To provide an additional amount of insurance when damages for which the insured is held liable exceed the per occurrence limit in an underlying liability policy
   (2) To pay liability claims that are not covered in full by an underlying policy because the aggregate limit in the underlying liability policy has been depleted or exhausted
   (3) To cover claims that are outside the scope of the coverage of underlying policies

3-10. Parties involved in a surety bond have the following roles:
   a. Obligee—The party to whom the principal and surety are obligated
   b. Principal—Obligated to perform in some way for the benefit of the obligee
   c. Surety—Guarantees to the obligee that the principal will fulfill the underlying obligations

3-11. The following are the major categories of surety bonds:
   a. Contract bonds—guarantee the performance of public or private contracts
   b. License and permit bonds—required by federal, state, or municipal governments as prerequisites to engaging in certain business activities
   c. Court bonds—prescribed by statute
   d. Miscellaneous bonds—often support private relationships and unique business needs

3-12. Nonfiled inland marine insurance uses forms and rates that are not filed with regulatory authorities. Being exempt from filing requirements allows insurers to tailor inland marine forms and rates to fit particular loss exposures that are not adequately insured under other property forms.

3-13. Crime insurance complements commercial property insurance because most commercial property forms exclude coverage for money and securities.

3-14. Some consider loss control services to be the most valuable aspects of equipment breakdown insurance. Insurers have specialty engineers who perform regular inspections of the equipment. Their recommendations help the organization safely operate the equipment.

3-15. Difference in conditions insurance was designed as a means of providing "all-risks" coverage to organizations whose property insurance provided only basic or broad form causes of loss. More often, it is purchased to provide the following:
   • Flood and earthquake coverage for loss exposures that are not covered in other property policies
   • Excess limits over flood and earthquake coverages included in other property policies
   • Coverage for loss exposures not covered in other property policies
   • Coverage for overseas property

3-16. Shop and Gas could have any number commercial insurance needs. However, it would most likely need the following types of insurance: property insurance, general liability insurance, workers' compensation and employers' liability insurance, and auto insurance.

Educational Objective 4

4-1. The advantages of using insurance as a risk financing technique include the following:
   • Reduces financial uncertainty from accidental losses
   • Provides access to claim handling services
   • Offers access to risk control services
   • Satisfies creditor requirements
   • Satisfies legal requirements
   • Satisfies business requirements
   • Offers tax-deductible premiums

- Is flexible in design
- Is easy to exit

The disadvantages of using insurance as a risk financing technique include the following:
- Insurance premiums include insurer expenses, profits, and risk charges.
- Insurance premiums diminish cash flows.
- Insurance coverage is not a complete transfer of hazard risk.
- Insurance price and availability at desired terms and conditions fluctuate.

4-2. The value of insurance services commonly provided to policyholders includes:
  a. Claim-handling expertise has value because insurers are adept at handling volumes of claims, complex claims, and claims requiring special expertise. In addition, insurer claim-handling services are considered to be impartial.
  b. Risk control efforts have value and might result in expense savings for an organization because an insurer's efforts are aimed at reducing the frequency or severity of losses or making losses more predictable.

4-3. Underwriting cycles indicate the following trends in insurance pricing and availability:
  a. A soft market underwriting cycle is characterized by low rates, relaxed underwriting, and underwriting losses for insurers.
  b. A hard market underwriting cycle is characterized by high rates, restrictive underwriting, and underwriting gains for insurers.

4-4. a. Local Municipality's risk management professional may argue that insurance is the preferred approach because the municipality's residents value the reduction in uncertainty from accidental losses that insurance provides, and insurance offers access to risk control services that the municipality needs but may have difficulty affording if those services were to be purchased separately.
  b. Local Municipality's risk management professional may determine that retention is the preferred approach to handling risk because the municipality is not only paying for its own losses, but also bearing part of the insurer's costs such as insurer expenses, profits, and risk charges. Additionally, the advance premium payment made by the municipality diminishes the amount of cash it has to satisfy other cash needs.

Direct Your Learning

Insurance Plan Design

Educational Objectives

After learning the content of this assignment, you should be able to:

1. Describe the importance and contents of insurance binders.
2. Describe the physical construction of insurance policies.
3. Summarize the effect of each of the following common policy provisions:
   - Declarations
   - Definitions
   - Insuring agreement
   - Conditions
   - Exclusions
   - Miscellaneous provisions
4. Describe the types of property and liability deductibles.
5. Explain how large deductible plans operate.
6. Describe the role of excess liability insurance in providing an organization with adequate liability coverage limits.
7. Describe the role of umbrella liability insurance in providing an organization with adequate liability coverage limits.
8. Define or describe each of the Key Words and Phrases for this assignment.

Study Materials

Required Reading:
- Risk Financing
  - Chapter 3

Study Aids:
- SMART Online Practice Exam
- SMART Study Aids
  - Review Notes and Flash Cards—Assignment 3

Outline

- **Insurance Binders**
- **Physical Construction of Insurance Policies**
    - A. Self-Contained Versus Modular Policies
    - B. Preprinted Forms
        1. Standard Forms
        2. Nonstandard Forms
    - C. Manuscript Forms
    - D. Related Documents
- **Common Policy Provisions**
    - A. Declarations
    - B. Definitions
    - C. Insuring Agreements
        1. Scope of Insuring Agreements
        2. Insuring Agreements for Extended, Additional, or Supplemental Coverages
        3. Other Provisions That Function as Insuring Agreements
    - D. Conditions
    - E. Exclusions
        1. Eliminate Coverage for Uninsurable Loss Exposures
        2. Assist in Managing Moral and Morale Hazards
        3. Reduce the Likelihood of Coverage Duplications
        4. Eliminate Coverages Not Needed by the Typical Insured
        5. Eliminate Coverages Requiring Special Treatment
        6. Assist in Keeping Premiums Reasonable
    - F. Miscellaneous Provisions
- **Deductibles**
    - A. Property Deductibles
    - B. Liability Deductibles
- **Large Deductible Plans**
    - A. Purpose and Operation of Large Deductible Plans
    - B. Advantages and Disadvantages of Large Deductible Plans
- **Excess Liability Insurance**
    - A. Following-Form Excess Liability Policies
    - B. Self-Contained Excess Liability Policies
    - C. Combination Excess Liability Policies
    - D. Specific and Aggregate (or Stop Loss) Excess Liability Insurance
- **Umbrella Liability Insurance**
    - A. Basic Functions of Umbrella Liability Policies
    - B. Self-Insured Retention
    - C. Exclusions Omitted From an Umbrella Liability Policy
    - D. Umbrella Liability Policy Exclusions Less Restrictive Than the Underlying Coverage
    - E. Umbrella Liability Policy Exclusions More Restrictive Than the Underlying Coverage
- **Structuring a Liability Insurance Program**
- **Case Studies in Insurance Plan Design**
    - A. Coastal Warehouse Company
    - B. Baby Products Manufacturing Company
- **Summary**

 Actively capture information by using the open space in the SMART Review Notes to write out key concepts. Putting information into your own words is an effective way to push that information into your memory.

For each assignment, you should define or describe each of the Key Words and Phrases and answer each of the Review and Application Questions.

> # Educational Objective 1
> **Describe the importance and contents of insurance binders.**

Key Word or Phrase
Insurance binder (p. 3.3)

Review Questions

1-1. Explain the purpose of an insurance binder. (p. 3.3)

1-2. Explain why it is important for the risk management professional to review the information contained in the insurance binder. (p. 3.4)

1-3. Identify the key items of information contained in a binder. (p. 3.4)

Application Question

1-4. Unhappy with her commercial property insurer, Retail Store's owner has purchased replacement coverage through a new insurance agent and another insurer. The new agent has binding authority with the insurer and has issued a binder. Before the policy can be issued, the business is destroyed by a fire. Explain the basis on which Retail Store's claim will likely be settled.

Educational Objective 2
Describe the physical construction of insurance policies.

Key Words and Phrases

Monoline policy (p. 3.4)

Package policy (p. 3.4)

Coverage part (p. 3.6)

Self-contained policy (p. 3.6)

Endorsement (p. 3.6)

Modular policy (p. 3.6)

Standard insurance form (p. 3.9)

Nonstandard form (p. 3.9)

Manuscript form (p. 3.10)

Review Questions

2-1. Describe the components that may be included in a coverage part of an insurance policy. (p. 3.6)

2-2. Identify the purpose of a policy endorsement. (p. 3.6)

2-3. Identify the advantages of using the modular approach to policy construction. (p. 3.8)

2-4. Describe the benefits of working with standard forms. (p. 3.9)

2-5. Describe the (a) benefit(s) and (b) drawback(s) of using manuscript forms. (p. 3.10)

Application Question

2-6. Storage Warehouse's (SW) insurance claim is denied because the damaged warehouse was vacant longer than the policy permitted. SW's risk management professional produces a handwritten endorsement from the insurer's underwriter that states the vacancy period has been extended by the insurer to include the period in which the loss occurred. In this case, which document takes precedence and why?

Educational Objective 3

Summarize the effect of each of the following common policy provisions:
- Declarations
- Definitions
- Insuring agreement
- Conditions
- Exclusions
- Miscellaneous provisions

Key Words and Phrases

Policy provision (p. 3.13)

Insuring agreement (p. 3.17)

Condition (p. 3.21)

Review Questions

3-1. Briefly describe the six categories of property-casualty insurance policy provisions. (pp. 3.13–3.27)

3-2. Describe how to recognize which words in a policy have a special definition. (pp. 3.14–3.17)

3-3. Describe how exclusions, definitions, and other policy provisions are used to modify coverage in the following insuring agreement categories: (p. 3.17)

   a. Comprehensive insuring agreements

   b. Limited or single-purpose insuring agreements

3-4. Explain the effect that policy conditions may have on the insured's ability to recover on a loss from its insurer. (p. 3.21)

3-5. Identify six purposes of exclusions in insurance policies. (p. 3.22)

Application Question

3-6. Music Recording Company is concerned that undefined terms and phrases in its insurance policies will not be interpreted in its favor in light of new, Internet-based technologies. Explain how undefined words and phrases will be interpreted if their meaning is disputed.

Educational Objective 4
Describe the types of property and liability deductibles.

Key Words and Phrases
Deductible (p. 3.27)

Flat, or straight, deductible (p. 3.28)

Disappearing, or franchise, deductible (p. 3.28)

Percentage deductible (p. 3.28)

Aggregate annual deductible (p. 3.28)

3.10 Risk Financing—ARM 56

Per claim deductible (p. 3.29)

Per accident/occurrence deductible (p. 3.29)

Waiting period deductible (p. 3.29)

Review Questions

4-1. Explain how deductibles support the economical operation of insurance. (p. 3.27)

4-2. Briefly describe how the following types of deductibles are applied in property insurance policies. (p. 3.28)
   a. Flat, or straight, deductible

   b. Disappearing, or franchise, deductible

c. Percentage deductible

d. Aggregate annual deductible

4-3. Briefly describe how the following types of liability deductibles are applied in insurance policies: (p. 3.29)
   a. Per claim deductible

   b. Per accident/occurrence deductible

   c. Waiting period deductible

Application Question

4-4. An earthquake causes a $3 million property loss to Office Building Company's (OBC) building that was valued at $5 million before the loss. OBC's property insurance policy has a $4.5 million coverage limit and contains a percentage deductible (10 percent) that applies to the property's value at the time of the loss. What is the dollar amount of OBC's deductible?

Educational Objective 5
Explain how large deductible plans operate.

Key Words and Phrases
Large deductible plan (p. 3.30)

Residual market loading (p. 3.31)

Review Questions

5-1. Explain how the use of large deductible plans enables an organization to lower its cost of risk. (p. 3.30)

5-2. Explain the difference in operation between large deductible plans and self-insured retention (SIR). (p. 3.31)

5-3. Identify two reasons why reducing the premium reduces costs of risk under a large deductible plan. (p. 3.31)

Application Question

5-4. In-Ground Pool Installation Company's (IGPIC) insurance program includes a general liability policy with a large deductible of $100,000. This policy provides loss adjustment expenses that are outside the deductible and that are shared proportionately based on the size of the loss. IGPIC's insurer settles a $1 million loss for which it incurs $300,000 in legal fees. What is IGPIC's share of the insurer's legal fees?

Educational Objective 6
Describe the role of excess liability insurance in providing an organization with adequate liability coverage limits.

Key Words and Phrases
Excess liability insurance (p. 3.33)

Following-form excess liability policy (p. 3.34)

Self-contained excess liability policy (p. 3.34)

Combination excess liability policy (p. 3.34)

Specific excess liability insurance policy (p. 3.35)

Aggregate, or stop loss, excess liability insurance policy (p. 3.35)

Review Questions
6-1. Identify two basic functions of excess liability provisions. (p. 3.33)

6-2. List the three basic excess liability policy forms above an underlying liability policy. (p. 3.33)

6-3. Describe coverage differences in using the following types of excess liability forms: (pp. 3.34–3.35)

   a. Following-form excess liability policy

   b. Self-contained excess liability policy

   c. Combination excess liability policy

   d. Specific and aggregate excess liability insurance

Application Question

6-4. International Conglomerate's (IC) risk financing program includes a $1 million self-insured retention (SIR) for its auto liability and general liability loss exposures. IC also has a SIR for its workers' compensation program, but IC's retention is limited to $250,000. IC has purchased separate specific excess liability polices for each of those loss exposures. Each specific excess policy provides a $1 million limit. IC also has a $2 million annual aggregate excess liability policy. Based on this information, diagram IC's risk financing plan.

Educational Objective 7

Describe the role of umbrella liability insurance in providing an organization with adequate liability coverage limits.

Key Words and Phrases

Umbrella liability insurance policy (p. 3.36)

Drop-down coverage (p. 3.37)

Buffer layer (p. 3.39)

Review Questions

7-1. Identify the three basic functions of an umbrella liability policy. (p. 3.36)

7-2. Describe circumstances in which self-insured retention does not apply in claims not covered by the insured's underlying policies. (p. 3.37)

7-3. Identify underlying policy exclusions that provide broader coverage that are frequently omitted from umbrella liability policies. (p. 3.37)

7-4. Describe how the risk management professional determines how an organization's liability coverage is structured. (pp. 3.38–3.39)

Application Question

7-5. Restaurant and Bar's (RB) sales are evenly split between food and alcoholic beverages. RB has purchased an umbrella liability insurance policy to address its liability loss exposure. Explain why RB's umbrella coverage may not satisfy its needs. (p. 3.37)

Answers to Assignment 3 Questions

NOTE: These answers are provided to give students a basic understanding of acceptable types of responses. They often are not the only valid answers and are not intended to provide an exhaustive response to the questions.

Educational Objective 1

1-1. The purpose of an insurance binder is to provide insurance coverage until a written policy is issued. The binder serves as evidence of insurance until the actual policy is issued.

1-2. It is important for the risk management professional to review the information contained in the insurance binder because the insurer's claim representative may use the binder to settle losses until the policy is issued. The binder contains much of the final policy's organization-specific information.

1-3. Key items of information contained in a binder include the following:
- Name of the insured, insurer, and producer
- Insurance coverage effective and expiration dates
- Coverages and limits information by type of insurance
- Mortgagee and loss payee information

1-4. If Retail Store incurs any claims before the issuance of the policy, they will be settled using the information contained in the binder.

Educational Objective 2

2-1. Components included in a coverage part of an insurance policy may include the following:
- Declarations page—applies only to that coverage part
- One or more coverage forms—contain insuring agreements, exclusions, and other policy provisions
- Applicable endorsements—modify the terms of the coverage form(s) to fit the coverage needs of the particular insured

2-2. The purpose of a policy endorsement is to add, clarify, restrict, or remove coverage provided by the original insurance policy.

2-3. The following are advantages of using the modular approach to policy construction:
- Carefully designed and coordinated provisions minimize the possibility of gaps and overlaps.
- Consistent terminology, definitions, and policy language make coverage interpretation easier for the insured organization.
- Fewer forms are required to meet a wide range of needs.
- Insurers often give a package discount when several coverages are included in the same policy.

2-4. Standard forms are widely understood, and many of them have been subjected to litigation, which has added further clarity to their meaning. Furthermore, most risk management professionals have more experience working with preprinted standard forms than with most other forms.

2-5. a. The primary benefit of manuscript forms is that they can be specifically drafted or selected for a particular need.

b. The primary drawback of manuscript forms is that they may be difficult for the risk management professional to interpret. Manuscript forms do not have the same history of court interpretations on which risk management professionals can rely.

2-6. An endorsement takes precedence over any conflicting terms in the policy to which it is attached. Consequently, Storage Warehouse's policy would provide coverage. In most instances, the insurer would have maintained a copy or a notation of the endorsement.

Educational Objective 3

3-1. The six categories of property-liability insurance policy provisions are as follows:
   (1) Declarations—contains information declared by the insured on the application and information unique to a particular policy
   (2) Definitions—defines terms used throughout the entire policy or form
   (3) Insuring agreements—statements that the insurer will, under certain circumstances, make a payment or provide a service
   (4) Conditions—provision that qualifies an otherwise enforceable promise of the insurer
   (5) Exclusions—clarifies the coverages granted by the insurer
   (6) Miscellaneous provisions—provisions that deal with the relationship between the insured and the insurer, help establish working procedures for implementing coverage, but do not have the force of conditions

3-2. Policies typically use boldface type or quotation marks to distinguish words and phrases that have special meaning and are defined elsewhere in the policy.

3-3. Exclusions, definitions, and other policy provisions modify coverage in the following insuring agreement categories:
   a. Comprehensive, all-purpose insuring agreements—Coverage is clarified and narrowed by exclusions, definitions, and other policy provisions.
   b. Limited or single-purpose insuring agreements—Exclusions, definitions, and other policy provisions serve to clarify and narrow coverage, but also may broaden coverage.

3-4. A policy condition qualifies an otherwise enforceable promise of the insurer. Insureds that fail to satisfy the conditions of the policy may release the insurer from any obligation to perform some or all of its otherwise enforceable promises.

3-5. Six purposes of exclusions in insurance policies are as follows:
   (1) To eliminate coverage for uninsurable loss exposures
   (2) To assist in managing moral and morale hazards
   (3) To reduce the likelihood of coverage duplication
   (4) To eliminate coverages not needed by the typical insured
   (5) To eliminate coverages requiring special treatment
   (6) To assist in keeping premiums reasonable

3-6. Music Recording Company (MRC) may be able interpret undefined words and phrases in its insurance policies with the following rules:
   • Everyday words are given their ordinary meanings.

- Technical words are given their technical meanings.
- Words with an established legal meaning are given their legal meanings.
- Consideration is also given to the local, cultural, and trade-usage meanings of words, if applicable.

Educational Objective 4

4-1. Deductibles support the economical operation of insurance by allowing an insured organization to obtain the risk transfer it needs while retaining those losses it can safely absorb.

4-2. Deductibles are applied as follows in property insurance policies:
   a. Flat, or straight, deductible—Stated in a dollar amount and usually applies per occurrence, regardless of the number of items of covered property that are damaged.
   b. Disappearing, or franchise, deductible—Decreases in amount as the amount of loss increases, and disappears entirely after a specified amount of loss is surpassed.
   c. Percentage deductible—Stated as a specified percentage, as a percentage of the loss, percentage of the amount of insurance, or specified percentage of the value of the affected property.
   d. Aggregate annual deductible—Limits the total amount retained during a year. After the aggregate annual deductible has been met, the insurer provides first-dollar coverage on all subsequent losses.

4-3. Liability deductibles are applied as follows in insurance policies:
   a. Per claim deductible—applies to all damages sustained by any one person or organization as a result of one occurrence
   b. Per accident/occurrence deductible—applies only once to the total of all claims paid arising out of one accident or occurrence
   c. Waiting period deductible—payable after a specified time period

4-4. OBC would retain $500,000 (10 percent of $5 million). This percentage deductible applies to the property's value at the time of the loss.

Educational Objective 5

5-1. By using large deductible plans, organizations can lower cost of risk because they are able to pay a reduced insurance premium while retaining losses below the deductible level. In addition, organizations are able to defer cash outflows for accidental losses.

5-2. The difference in operation between large deductible plans and self-insured retention (SIR) includes the following:
   - With SIR, the insured organization is responsible for adjusting and paying its own losses up to the SIR amount. This task is frequently outsourced to an independent claim adjusting organization.
   - With a large deductible plan, the insurer adjusts and pays all claims for loss, even those below the deductible level, and seeks reimbursement from the insured.

5-3. Reducing premiums reduce costs for the following reasons:
   (1) States impose various charges, such as premium taxes and residual market loadings.
   (2) An insurance premium includes charges for the insurer's overhead costs and profit.

5-4. In-Ground Pool Installation Company (IGPIC) will share in 10 percent of the legal fees, or $30,000, because the deductible amount was 10 percent of the amount paid by the insurer.

Educational Objective 6

6-1. The following are two basic functions of excess liability provisions:
   (1) To provide additional liability limits above the each occurrence/accident limits of the insured's underlying liability policies
   (2) To take the place of the underlying liability insurance when underlying aggregate liability limits have been exhausted

6-2. The three basic excess liability policy forms above an underlying liability policy are
   (1) A following form subject to the same provisions as the underlying liability policy
   (2) A self-contained policy subject to its own provisions
   (3) A combination of the two types

6-3. The different types of excess liability forms offer the following coverages:
   a. Following-form excess liability policy—covers a liability loss that exceeds the underlying policy limits only if the underlying insurance covers the loss
   b. Self-contained excess liability policy—subject to its own provisions only, so coverage applies only to the extent described in the policy
   c. Combination excess liability policy—incorporates the provisions of the underlying policy and then modifies those provisions with additional conditions or exclusions in the excess policy
   d. Specific and aggregate excess liability insurance—requires the insured organization to retain a stipulated amount of liability loss from the first dollar for all losses resulting from a single occurrence or accident

6-4. A diagram of IC's risk financing plan is as follows:

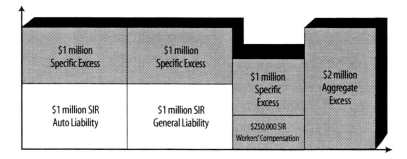

Educational Objective 7

7-1. The three basic functions of an umbrella liability policy are as follows:

(1) To provide additional limits above the per occurrence limits of the insured's underlying liability policies

(2) To take the place of the underlying liability insurance when underlying aggregate limits are exhausted

(3) To cover some claims that the insured organization's underlying liability policies do not cover

7-2. Self-insured retention normally does not apply in claims not covered by the insured's underlying policies in the following circumstances:

- When paying the excess amount of a loss that the underlying liability policy covers
- When dropping down to pay a loss because the underlying policy's aggregate liability limit has been exhausted

7-3. Underlying policy exclusions to broaden coverage that are frequently omitted from umbrella liability policies include the following:

- Liquor liability exclusion of a general liability policy
- Employers' liability insurance exclusion of accidents occurring outside the U.S. or Canada
- Employers' liability insurance exclusion of injury to persons subject to the Federal Employers' Liability Act, the Jones Act, and similar laws permitting employees to sue their employers
- Employers' liability insurance exclusion of injury to persons knowingly employed in violation of law

7-4. When structuring an organization's liability coverage, the risk management professional must evaluate the adequacy of each underlying layer and determine how much additional excess or umbrella liability coverage needs to be purchased.

7-5. Many umbrella liability insurance polices exclude liquor liability. Consequently, Restaurant and Bar has a loss exposure that is not insured beyond the limits of its general liability policy limits.

Direct Your Learning

Forecasting Accidental Losses and Risk Financing Needs

Educational Objectives

After learning the content of this assignment, you should be able to:

1. Describe the steps in forecasting expected losses.
2. Explain how to forecast the probable variation from expected losses.
3. Explain how loss forecasts can be used to estimate cash flow needs.
4. Explain how loss forecasts can be used to:
   - Budget for retained losses
   - Evaluate alternative retention levels
   - Evaluate insurer premium charges
   - Update accounting reserves for retained losses
5. Given a case, forecast expected losses and estimate the net present value of cash flow needs.
6. Define or describe each of the Key Words and Phrases for this assignment.

Study Materials

Required Reading:
- Risk Financing
  - Chapter 4

Study Aids:
- SMART Online Practice Exam
- SMART Study Aids
  - Review Notes and Flash Cards—Assignment 4

Outline

- **The Tarnton Company Case Study**
- **Part 1: Forecasting Expected Losses**
    - A. Step 1: Collect and Organize Past Data
        1. Loss Data
        2. Exposure Data
    - B. Step 2: Limit Individual Losses
    - C. Step 3: Apply Loss Development and Trend Factors to the Data
        1. Loss Development
        2. Loss Trend Factors
    - D. Step 4: Forecast Losses
        1. Compare Past Losses to Past Exposures
        2. Estimate Exposures
        3. Calculate Expected Losses
        4. Use Increased Limit Factor Tables
- **Part 2: Forecasting Probable Variation From Expected Loss**
    - A. Frequency Probability Distribution
    - B. Severity Probability Distribution
    - C. Total Loss Probability Distribution
    - D. Probability Intervals
- **Part 3: Estimating Cash Flow Needs**
    - A. Estimates of Loss Payout Patterns
    - B. Usefulness of Present Value Analysis
    - C. Net Present Value Analysis Applied to Loss Payouts
- **Using the Information Provided by Loss Forecasts**
    - A. Budget for Retained Losses
    - B. Evaluate Alternative Retention Levels
    - C. Evaluate Insurer Premium Charges
    - D. Update Accounting Reserves for Retained Losses
- **Summary**

Use the SMART Online Practice Exams to test your understanding of the course material. You can review questions over a single assignment or multiple assignments, or you can take an exam over the entire course. The questions are scored, and you are shown your results. (You score essay exams yourself.)

For each assignment, you should define or describe each of the Key Words and Phrases and answer each of the Review and Application Questions.

Educational Objective 1
Describe the steps in forecasting expected losses.

Key Words and Phrases

Paid losses (p. 4.6)

Loss reserves (p. 4.6)

Loss adjustment expense reserves (p. 4.6)

Incurred losses (p. 4.6)

Loss development (p. 4.6)

Loss payout pattern (p. 4.6)

Exposure unit (p. 4.8)

Increased limit factor tables (p. 4.9)

Trend factors (p. 4.11)

Loss development factors (p. 4.11)

Ultimate loss development factor (p. 4.11)

Review Questions

1-1. Describe the three parts of the accidental loss forecasting process an organization uses to forecast and budget its risk financing costs. (p. 4.3)

1-2. Identify the four steps a risk management professional should complete to prepare a forecast of expected losses. (p. 4.5)

1-3. Identify the past loss data required to make an accurate loss forecast. (p. 4.6)

1-4. Explain the purpose of limiting losses when forecasting expected losses. (p. 4.8)

Application Question

1-5. Listed below are the amounts paid-to-date and the current loss reserves for six liability claims incurred in 20X0 and evaluated as of 6/30/20X1, eighteen months after the beginning of the calendar year 20X0.

Claim Evaluation as of 6/20/20X1

20X0 Claim	Paid Losses	Loss Reserves	Incurred Losses
A	$46,000	$90,000	
B	10,000	0	
C	15,000	11,000	
D	4,000	1,000	
E	87,000	50,000	
F	14,000	30,000	
Totals			

a. Using this information, what is the total estimated value of incurred losses for the six claims as of the 6/30/20X1 evaluation date?

b. What is the estimated value of incurred claims if each claim is limited to the following:

(1) ≤ $20,000

(2) ≤ $50,000

Educational Objective 2
Explain how to forecast the probable variation from expected losses.

Key Words and Phrases

Frequency probability distribution (p. 4.23)

Severity probability distribution (p. 4.23)

Total probability distribution (p. 4.23)

Expected value (p. 4.24)

Review Questions

2-1. Describe the three types of probability distributions the analysis of an organization's past loss frequency and severity outcomes yields. (p. 4.22)

2-2. Describe how an organization may use probability distributions to measure the effectiveness of a risk control technique. (p. 4.23)

2-3. Describe how a risk management professional calculates the following values when developing forecasts from past losses: (pp. 4.24–4.27)
    a. Expected value

    b. Mean (average) severity

    c. Mean of a frequency distribution

Application Question

2-4. Using the following data, calculate the total mean severity:

Severity Range	Mean Severity	Probability	Mean Severity × Probability
$ 5,000–$ 9,999	$	0.40	$
$10,000–$14,999	$	0.30	$
$15,000–$19,999	$	0.20	$
$20,000–$24,999	$	0.07	$
$25,000 and over	$	0.03	$
Total		1.00	$

Educational Objective 3
Explain how loss forecasts can be used to estimate cash flow needs.

Review Questions

3-1. Identify the elements an organization should consider when developing a projection of its cash flow needs. (p. 4.29)

3-2. Identify the data used by an organization to develop loss payout patterns. (p. 4.30)

3-3. Identify how an organization may use present value analysis. (pp. 4.31–4.32)

Application Question

3-4. Using the data below, calculate the cumulative percentage paid for each accident year.

Accident Year	Months After Beginning of Accident Year	Paid Losses (Limited to $25,000)	Estimated Ultimate Incurred Losses	Cumulative Percentage Paid
X1	60	$350,000	$400,000	%
X2	48	$250,000	$325,000	%
X3	36	$100,000	$235,000	%
X4	24	$ 25,000	$100,000	%
X5	12	$ 10,000	$ 55,000	%

> **Educational Objective 4**
>
> Explain how loss forecasts can be used to:
>
> - Budget for retained losses
> - Evaluate alternative retention levels
> - Evaluate insurer premium charges
> - Update accounting reserves for retained losses

Review Questions

4-1. Identify how a risk management professional may use the information generated by loss forecasts. (pp. 4.34–4.37)

4-2. Identify the assumptions on which accurate loss forecast calculations depend. (p. 4.34)

4-3. Explain why a risk charge is often built into an insured's premium. (p. 4.36)

Application Question

4-4. Using the following data, determine whether insurer's premium charge is reasonable:

Total expected losses	$300,000
Total losses retained with a $25,000 deductible	$100,000
Insurer expenses	$20,000
Quoted premium	$235,000

Educational Objective 5

Given a case, forecast expected losses and estimate the net present value of cash flow.

Application Question

5-1. Using the data below, calculate the following period-to-period loss development factors:

Months of Development

Year	12	24	36	48	60	72 (Ultimate)
X1	10,000	10,200	10,300	10,350	10,375	10,375
X2	12,000	12,300	12,500	12,600	12,650	12,650
X3	14,000	14,500	14,750	14,850	14,900	
X4	16,000	16,600	16,900	17,050		
X5	18,000	18,800	19,200			
X6	20,000	21,000				
X7	22,000					

Period-to-Period Loss Development Factors

Year	12 to 24	25 to 36	37 to 48	49 to 60	61 to 72 Ultimate
X1					
X2					
X3					
X4					
X5					
X6					
Average					

a. 60 months to ultimate

b. 48 months to ultimate

c. 36 months to ultimate

d. 24 months to ultimate

e. 12 months to ultimate

Answers to Assignment 4 Questions

NOTE: These answers are provided to give students a basic understanding of acceptable types of responses. They often are not the only valid answers and are not intended to provide an exhaustive response to the questions.

Educational Objective 1

1-1. The following are the three parts of the accidental loss forecasting process:
   (1) Part 1—Forecast expected losses by calculating an estimate of the expected (average) losses for the upcoming year based on past data.
   (2) Part 2—Forecast probable variation from expected losses by using probability distributions and probability intervals.
   (3) Part 3—Estimate cash flow needs by estimating the timing of loss payments.

1-2. A risk management professional should complete the following four steps to prepare a forecast of expected losses:
   (1) Collect and organize past data.
   (2) Limit individual losses.
   (3) Apply loss development and trend factors to the data.
   (4) Forecast losses.

1-3. Past loss data required to make an accurate loss forecast include paid losses, loss reserves, and loss adjustment reserves.

1-4. Individual losses are limited so that the analysis focuses on the layer of losses that have sufficient frequency to be predictable and therefore retainable.

1-5. The historical data is used as follows to forecast losses:
   a. The total estimated value of incurred claims as of the 6/30/20X1 evaluation date equals the total of paid losses and loss reserves for each claim ($358,000), calculated as follows:

Claims Evaluation as of 6/30/20X1

Calendar 20X0 Claim	Paid Losses-to-Date	Loss Reserves	Incurred Losses
A	$46,000	$90,000	$136,000
B	10,000	0	10,000
C	15,000	11,000	26,000
D	4,000	1,000	5,000
E	87,000	50,000	137,000
F	14,000	30,000	44,000
Total	$176,000	$182,000	$358,000

b. The following is the estimated value of incurred claims:

(1) ≤ $20,000 per claim

Claim	Limited Claim (≤ $20,000)
A	$20,000
B	10,000
C	20,000
D	5,000
E	20,000
F	20,000
Total	$95,000

(2) ≤ $50,000 per claim

Claim	Limited Claim (≤ $50,000)
A	$50,000
B	10,000
C	26,000
D	5,000
E	50,000
F	44,000
Total	$185,000

Educational Objective 2

2-1. Analysis of an organization's past loss frequency and severity outcomes yields the following three types of probability distributions:

   (1) Frequency probability distribution—shows the probability of various numbers of losses over a certain time period

   (2) Severity probability distribution—shows the probability of various sizes of each individual loss

   (3) Total loss probability distribution—shows the probability of particular total loss outcomes for a given period

2-2. Effective risk control techniques should reduce actual loss frequency and severity compared to the probable loss frequency and severity indicated in the probability distribution.

2-3. A risk management professional calculates the following values when developing forecasts from past losses:

   a. Expected value—To calculate, multiply each possible outcome by its probability and sum the results.

   b. Mean (average) severity—To calculate, multiply the average severity outcome in each range by the probability of the losses falling within that range.

   c. Mean of a total loss distribution—To calculate, multiply the mean of the frequency distribution by the mean of the severity distribution.

2-4. The mean severity is calculated as follows:

Severity Range	Mean Severity	Probability	Mean Severity × Probability
$ 5,000 – $ 9,999	$ 7,500	0.40	$3,000
$10,000 – $14,999	$12,500	0.30	3,750
$15,000 – $19,999	$17,500	0.20	3,500
$20,000 – $24,999	$22,500	0.07	1,575
$25,000 and over	$25,000	0.03	750
Total		1.00	$12,575

Educational Objective 3

3-1. An organization should consider the estimated total cost of a risk financing plan and the expected timing of cash payments when developing a projection of its cash flow needs.

3-2. Loss payout patterns are projected based on an organization's own past payout patterns, industry data, or a combination of the two.

3-3. An organization may use present value analysis in the following ways:
- To reflect the interest that the budgeted funds will earn until losses are paid
- When evaluating alternative retention levels
- When evaluating the reasonableness of the insurer's premium charge
- When evaluating accounting reserves placed on past retained losses

3-4.

Accident Year	Months After Beginning of Accident Year	Paid Losses (Limited to $25,000)	Estimated Ultimate Incurred Losses	Cumulative Percentage Paid
X1	60	$350,000	$400,000	88%
X2	48	$250,000	$325,000	77%
X3	36	$100,000	$235,000	43%
X4	24	$25,000	$100,000	25%
X5	12	$10,000	$55,000	18%

Educational Objective 4

4-1. A risk management professional may use the information generated by loss forecasts for the following purposes:
- To budget for retained losses
- To evaluate alternative retention levels
- To evaluate insurer premium charges
- To update accounting reserves for retained losses that occurred in the past

4-2. Accurate loss forecast calculations depend on the following assumptions:
- Having past data that are considerable in quantity and relevant
- That the future will essentially be like the past

4-3 A risk charge is often built into an insured's premium because insured losses are subject to more variability than retained losses. The risk charge is built into the premium amount to cover any contingencies.

4-4. Whether the premium charge is reasonable can be determined by subtracting the total losses retained with a $25,000 deductible from the amount of total expected losses. This calculation yields $200,000 ($300,000 – $100,000). Before comparing this amount to the premium charge, the insurer's expenses must be added to yield $220,000 ($200,000 + $20,000). The quoted premium is $15,000 higher than the estimate, which suggests that the insurer price may be lower.

Educational Objective 5

5-1.   Period-to-Period Loss Development Factors (rounded)

Year	12 to 24	25 to 36	37 to 48	49 to 60	61 to 72 Ultimate
X1	1.020	1.010	1.005	1.002	1.000
X2	1.025	1.016	1.008	1.004	1.000
X3	1.036	1.017	1.007	1.003	
X4	1.038	1.018	1.009		
X5	1.044	1.021			
X6	1.050				
Average	1.036	1.016	1.007	1.003	1.000

a. 60 months to ultimate $1.000 = 1.000$
b. 48 months to ultimate $1.003 \times 1.000 = 1.003$
c. 36 months to ultimate $1.007 \times 1.003 \times 1.000 = 1.010$
d. 24 months to ultimate $1.016 \times 1.007 \times 1.003 \times 1.000 = 1.026$
e. 12 months to ultimate $1.036 \times 1.016 \times 1.007 \times 1.003 \times 1.000 = 1.063$

Direct Your Learning

Self-Insurance Plans

Educational Objectives

After learning the content of this assignment, you should be able to:

1. Describe the purpose and operation of self-insurance plans.
2. Describe the two types of self-insurance plans.
3. Describe the administration of individual self-insurance plans.
4. Describe the advantages and disadvantages of self-insurance plans.
5. Given a case, justify a self-insurance plan that can meet an organization's risk financing needs.
6. Define or describe each of the Key Words and Phrases for this assignment.

Study Materials

Required Reading:
- Risk Financing
  - Chapter 5

Study Aids:
- SMART Online Practice Exam
- SMART Study Aids
  - Review Notes and Flash Cards—Assignment 5

Outline

- **Purpose and Operation of Self-Insurance Plans**
- **Types of Self-Insurance Plans**
    - A. Individual Self-Insurance Plans
    - B. Group Self-Insurance Plans
- **Administration of Individual Self-Insurance Plans**
    - A. Funding
    - B. Recordkeeping
    - C. Claim Settlement
    - D. Loss Reserves
    - E. Litigation Management
    - F. Regulatory Filings
    - G. Taxes, Assessments, and Fees
    - H. Excess Liability Insurance
- **Advantages and Disadvantages of Self-Insurance Plans**
    - A. Advantages
    - B. Disadvantages
- **Case Studies in Self-Insurance Plans**
    - A. Carpentry Contractor Company
    - B. Metal Products Manufacturing Company
- **Summary**

 The SMART Online Practice Exams product contains a final practice exam. You should take this exam only when you have completed your study of the entire course. Take this exam under simulated exam conditions. It will be your best indicator of how well prepared you are.

Self-Insurance Plans 5.3

For each assignment, you should define or describe each of the Key Words and Phrases and answer each of the Review and Application Questions.

> ## Educational Objective 1
> Describe the purpose and operation of self-insurance plans.

Key Words and Phrases

Self-insurance (p. 5.3)

Informal retention (p. 5.3)

Review Questions

1-1. Contrast self-insurance and informal retention. (p. 5.3)

1-2. Explain why an organization using self-insurance usually also purchases excess liability insurance. (p. 5.4)

1-3. Identify characteristics of organizations for which self-insurance is appropriate. (p. 5.4)

1-4. Identify loss exposures for which a self-insurance plan is well-suited. (pp. 5.4–5.5)

Application Question

1-5. Physicians Practice, frustrated with the availability and cost of medical malpractice insurance, is considering using self-insurance for this loss exposure. Evaluate whether self-insurance is appropriate for Physicians Practice.

Educational Objective 2
Describe the two types of self-insurance plans.

Key Words and Phrases
Individual self-insurance plan (p. 5.6)

Group self-insurance plan (p. 5.6)

Review Questions

2-1. Identify the two types of self-insurance plans. (p. 5.5)

2-2. Describe the conditions under which an organization can self-insure its loss exposures. (p. 5.6)

2-3. Describe how a group self-insurance plan helps an organization manage its cost of risk. (p. 5.6)

Application Question

2-4. Small Manufacturer (SM) has investigated self-insuring its workers' compensation loss exposure through an individual self-insurance plan. Explain how SM may be able to get some of the same benefits through group self-insurance.

Educational Objective 3
Describe the administration of individual self-insurance plans.

Key Words and Phrases
Third-party administrator (TPA) (p. 5.8)

Incurred but not reported (IBNR) losses (p. 5.9)

Review Questions

3-1. Identify the activities involved in the administration of an individual self-insurance plan. (p. 5.6)

3-2. List the activities that may be performed by a claim representative in the process of claim settlement. (p. 5.8)

3-3. Identify the conditions set forth by generally accepted accounting principles that require the establishment of a loss reserve. (p. 5.9)

3-4. Describe activities involved in litigation management. (p. 5.10)

3-5. Describe the effect of regulation on self-insured organizations. (p. 5.10)

3-6. Identify two approaches that states use to assess self-insured organizations. (p. 5.10)

Application Question

3-7. Bicycle Manufacturing Company (BMC) self-insures its general liability loss exposure. Based on its extensive loss history, BMC's management directs the establishment of a $5 million expense on its income statement as well as a liability on its balance sheet. BMC's certified public accountant (CPA) objects. What may be the basis of the CPA's objection?

Educational Objective 4
Describe the advantages and disadvantages of self-insurance plans.

Review Questions

4-1. List the major advantages of self-insurance plans. (pp. 5.11–5.12)

4-2. Explain how the use of a self-insurance plan encourages risk control. (p. 5.12)

4-3. Explain why an organization's long-run costs using self-insurance tend to be lower than the cost of transfer. (p. 5.12)

4-4. List the major disadvantages of self-insurance. (pp. 5.12–5.13)

4-5. Describe how the following bases of loss retention affect self-insured retention limits: (p. 5.13)

   a. Per occurrence basis

   b. Per accident basis

   c. Aggregate stop-loss basis

Application Question

4-6. National Home Builder (NHB) borrows millions of dollars annually from many financial institutions to finance its nationwide home building operation. Explain one advantage and one disadvantage NHB should consider when evaluating self-insurance as a way to finance its loss exposures.

5.10 Risk Financing—ARM 56

Educational Objective 5
Given a case, justify a self-insurance plan that can meet an organization's risk financing needs.

Application Question

5-1. Using the data below, calculate the present value disadvantage of deducting losses as the are paid rather than as they are incurred:

	Year 1	Year 2	Year 3	Year 4	Year 5	Total
Incurred Losses	$2,500,000					
Percent Paid		35%	20%	20%	15%	10%	100%
Amount Paid	$	$	$	$	$	$2,500,000
Loss Reserve	$	$	$	$	$	0	

	Year 1
Incurred Losses	$2,500,000
Savings in Taxes (30%)	$
Present Value Factor (10%)	0.9091
Present Value of Tax Savings	$

	Year 1	Year 2	Year 3	Year 4	Year 5	Total
Paid Losses	$	$	$	$	$	$2,500,000
Savings in Taxes (30%)	$	$	$	$	$	
Present Value Factor (10%)	0.9091	0.8264	0.7513	0.6830	0.6209	
Present Value of the Tax Savings	$	$	$	$	$	$

$ _____ Present value advantage of deducting losses as incurred
$ _____ Present value advantage of deducting losses as paid
$ _____ Present value disadvantage of deducting losses as paid rather than as incurred

Answers to Assignment 5 Questions

NOTE: These answers are provided to give students a basic understanding of acceptable types of responses. They often are not the only valid answers and are not intended to provide an exhaustive response to the questions.

Educational Objective 1

1-1. Self-insurance contrasts with informal retention because self-insurance is a loss retention plan in which an organization has decided to retain losses and requires that the organization keep records of its losses and maintain a formal system to pay for them. Informal retention is a type of retention in which an organization pays for its losses with its cash flow and/or current assets and does not involve formal payment procedures or methods for recording losses.

1-2. An organization using self-insurance usually also purchases excess liability insurance to limit the insured organization's exposure to loss to an acceptable level.

1-3. Organizations for which self-insurance is appropriate are those committed to risk control, able to tolerate risk retention, and those that are willing to devote capital and resources to the program's financing and administration.

1-4. Self insurance is well-suited for financing losses that are paid out over a period of time because it provides a cash flow benefit to the organization retaining its losses. Loss exposures that are well suited for a self-insurance plan include the following:
- Workers' compensation
- General liability
- Auto liability
- Auto physical damage
- Professional liability
- Flood
- Earthquake
- Healthcare benefits

1-5. Medical malpractice does not appear to be a loss exposure that is well-suited for self-insurance. Medical malpractice losses are generally infrequent and severe. Physicians Practice could potentially devote an excessive amount of capital and resources to the self-insurance program's financing and administration.

Educational Objective 2

2-1. The following are the two types of self-insurance plans:
(1) Individual self-insurance—used to address a number of loss exposures
(2) Group self-insurance—used only to address workers' compensation loss exposures and health care benefits

2-2. An organization is able to self-insure its loss exposures provided the state (or states) in which it operates permits self-insurance plans, and that the organization satisfies the state's requirements for self-insurers.

2-3. A group self-insurance plan helps an organization manage its cost of risk through economies of scale in administration, claim handling, and the purchase of excess liability insurance (or reinsurance).

2-4. Small Manufacturer (SM) can use group self-insurance to achieve many of the benefits afforded by individual self-insurance. A group self-insurance plan helps an organization that is too small to self-insure its loss exposures on its own. However, SM will not be able to self-insure other loss exposures, such as auto liability and general liability.

Educational Objective 3

3-1. Activities involved in the administration of a self-insurance plan include funding, recordkeeping, adjusting claims, reserving losses, managing litigation, making regulatory fillings, paying taxes, assessments, and fees; and maintaining excess insurance.

3-2. A claim representative may perform the following activities in the process of claim settlement:
- Investigate an accident scene
- Verify a claimant's statement of salary with the claimant's employer
- Compare a claimant's statement of the circumstances surrounding an accident with the police report's

3-3. The conditions set forth by generally accepted accounting principles that require the establishment of a loss reserve include the following:
(1) The loss occurred before the date of the financial statements.
(2) The amount that will be paid on the loss can be reasonably estimated.

3-4. The following activities are involved in litigation management:
- Evaluating and selecting defense lawyers
- Supervising defense lawyers during litigation
- Keeping records of defense lawyer costs
- Auditing legal bills and evaluating alternative fee-billing strategies

3-5. Self-insured organizations must make periodic filings with each state in which they seek to self-insure. Because each state has its own unique set of requirements, organizations that operate in multiple states may need to satisfy various requirements.

3-6. States may assess taxes based on a percentage of losses or as a percentage of what the organization would have paid in premium.

3-7. The basis of the CPA's objection may be that, under generally accepted accounting principles (GAAP), a self-insured organization cannot post loss reserves as a liability on its balance sheet and as an expense on its income statement if the losses have not occurred. If the organization were able to do this, it could later use those reserves and prematurely charged expenses to offset a year with higher-than-normal self-insured losses.

Educational Objective 4

4-1. The major advantages of self-insurance plans include the following:
- Control over claims

- Risk control
- Long-term cost savings
- Cash flow benefits

4-2. Using a self-insurance plan encourages risk control because the organization directly pays the cost of its own losses and therefore has an incentive to prevent and reduce them.

4-3. An organization's long-run costs using self-insurance tend to be lower than the cost of transfer because the organization does not have to contribute to an insurer's overhead costs and profits, does not have to pay an insurer's risk charge, and avoids premium taxes and residual market loadings.

4-4. Major disadvantages of self-insurance include the following:
- Uncertainty of retained loss outcomes
- Administrative requirements
- Deferral of tax deductions
- Contractual requirements

4-5. Self-insured retention limits are affected by the basis of loss retention in the following way:
   a. Per occurrence basis—A limit applies to the amount that the self-insured organization will pay for each loss occurrence, regardless of the number of claims (losses) arising from a single occurrence.
   b. Per accident basis—A limit applies to the amount that the self-insured organization will pay for each or accident, regardless of the number of claims (losses) arising from a single accident.
   c. Aggregate stop-loss basis—A limit applies to the amount that the self-insured organization will pay in total for all loss occurrences or accidents that take place during a period of time.

4-6. One advantage National Home Builder (NHB) should consider is the case flow benefit of self-insurance because of its extensive borrowing needs. One disadvantage it should consider, because it operates in multiple states, is that self-insurance may impose an administrative burden.

Educational Objective 5

5-1. The present value disadvantage of deducting losses as they are paid rather than as they are incurred is as follows:

	Year 1	Year 2	Year 3	Year 4	Year 5	Total
Incurred Losses	$2,500,000					
Percent Paid	35%	20%	20%	15%	10%	100%
Amount Paid	$875,000	$500,000	$500,000	$375,000	$250,000	$2,500,000
Loss Reserve	$1,625,000	$1,125,000	$625,000	$250,000	$0	

	Year 1
Incurred Losses	$2,500,000
Savings in Taxes (30%)	$750,000
Present Value Factor (10%)	0.9091
Present Value of Tax Savings	$681,825

5.14 Risk Financing—ARM 56

	Year 1	Year 2	Year 3	Year 4	Year 5	Total
Paid Losses	$875,000	$500,000	$500,000	$375,000	$250,000	
Savings in Taxes (30%)	$262,500	$150,000	$150,000	$112,500	$75,000	
Present Value Factor (10%)	0.9091	0.8264	0.7513	0.6830	0.6209	
Present Value of the Tax Savings	$238,639	$123,960	$112,695	$76,838	$46,568	$598,700

$681,825 Present value advantage of deducting losses as incurred
$598,700 Present value advantage of deducting losses as paid
$ 83,125 Present value disadvantage of deducting losses as paid rather than as incurred

Direct Your Learning

Retrospective Rating Plans

Educational Objectives

After learning the content of this assignment, you should be able to:

1. Describe the purpose and operation of retrospective rating plans.
2. Given a case, calculate the premium for a retrospective rating plan.
3. Describe the types of retrospective rating plans.
4. Describe the administration of retrospective rating plans.
5. Describe the advantages and disadvantages of retrospective rating plans.
6. Given a case, justify a retrospective rating plan that can meet an organization's risk financing needs.
7. Define or describe each of the Key Words and Phrases for this assignment.

Study Materials

Required Reading:
- Risk Financing
  - Chapter 6

Study Aids:
- SMART Online Practice Exam
- SMART Study Aids
  - Review Notes and Flash Cards—Assignment 6

Outline

- **Purpose and Operation of Retrospective Rating Plans**
  - A. Types of Losses Covered
  - B. Premium Determination
- **Calculation of Retrospective Rating Plan Insurance Premiums**
  - A. Retrospective Rating Insurance Premium Formula
  - B. Standard Premium
  - C. Basic Premium
  - D. Converted Losses
  - E. Excess Loss Premium
  - F. Tax Multiplier
  - G. Maximum and Minimum Premiums
  - H. Premium Adjustments
  - I. Retrospective Rating Plan Insurance Premium Calculation Case Study
- **Types of Retrospective Rating Plans**
  - A. Incurred Loss Retrospective Rating Plan
  - B. Paid Loss Retrospective Rating Plan
  - C. Comparison of Paid Loss With Incurred Loss Retrospective Rating Plans
- **Administration of Retrospective Rating Plans**
  - A. Collateral Requirements
  - B. Financial Accounting Issues
  - C. Tax Treatment
  - D. Exit Strategy
- **Advantages and Disadvantages of Retrospective Rating Plans**
  - A. Advantages
  - B. Disadvantages
- **Case Study in Retrospective Rating Plan Design**
- **Summary**

When you take the randomized full practice exams in the SMART Online Practice Exams product, you are using the same software you will use when you take the actual exam. Take advantage of your time and learn the features of the software now.

For each assignment, you should define or describe each of the Key Words and Phrases and answer each of the Review and Application Questions.

Educational Objective 1

Describe the purpose and operation of retrospective rating plans.

Key Words and Phrases

Retrospective rating plan (p. 6.3)

Experience rating (p. 6.5)

Maximum premium (p. 6.5)

Minimum premium (p. 6.6)

Loss limit (p. 6.6)

Review Questions

1-1. Explain why a retrospective rating plan is considered a hybrid risk financing plan. (p. 6.3)

1-2. Explain why a retrospective rating plan encourages an insured organization to control its losses. (p. 6.4)

1-3. Describe the types of loss exposures for which retrospective rating plans are commonly used. (p. 6.4)

1-4. Explain how the premium calculation under a retrospective rating plan differs from that under a guaranteed-cost insurance plan. (p. 6.5)

1-5. Describe how the following retrospective rating factors affect the loss amounts paid by an insurer: (pp. 6.5–6.6)
   a. Maximum premium

b. Minimum premium

c. Loss limit

1-6. Identify costs, other than retained losses, that are included in the premium under a retrospective rating plan. (pp. 6.6–6.7)

Application Question

1-7. The CFO of Large Manufacturer (LM) is struggling to understand LM's risk management professional's interest in using a retrospective rating plan. How may LM's risk management professional explain how a retrospective rating plan differs from its current experience-rated guaranteed-cost insurance plan?

Educational Objective 2

Given a case, calculate the premium for a retrospective rating plan.

Key Words and Phrases

Retrospective rating insurance premium formula (p. 6.8)

Standard premium (p. 6.8)

Basic premium (p. 6.9)

Insurance charge (p. 6.9)

Converted losses (p. 6.9)

Loss conversion factor (p. 6.9)

Excess loss premium (p. 6.10)

Tax multiplier (p. 6.10)

Review Questions

2-1. Provide the formula used to calculate the retrospective rating insurance premium. (p. 6.8)

2-2. Describe the following components of the retrospective rating insurance premium formula: (pp. 6.8–6.10)

   a. Standard premium

   b. Basic premium

   c. Converted losses

   d. Excess loss premium

   e. Tax multiplier

2-3. Explain the implication of the inclusion of a high loss conversion factor in an insurer's estimation of loss settlement costs. (p. 6.9)

Application Question

2-4. Assume XYZ Technology (XYZ) has the following cost factors for its incurred loss retrospective rating plan:

Policy Limit	$1,000,000 per occurrence
Standard Premium	$500,000
Discount	$25,000
Basic Premium	20%
Loss Conversion Factor	1.10
Loss Limit	$500,000 per occurrence
Excess Loss Premium	5%
Tax Multiplier	1.04
Maximum Premium	150%
Minimum Premium	40%

a. Calculate XYZ's basic premium.

b. Calculate XYZ's excess loss premium.

c. Calculate XYZ's maximum and minimum premiums.

Educational Objective 3

Describe the types of retrospective rating plans.

Key Words and Phrases

Incurred loss retrospective rating plan (p. 6.14)

Paid loss retrospective rating plan (p. 6.15)

Review Questions

3-1. Explain how an incurred loss retrospective rating plan differs from a paid loss retrospective rating plan. (pp. 6.14–6.15)

3-2. Describe the cash flow available to the insurer using incurred loss and paid loss retrospective rating plans. (pp. 6.14–6.15)

3-3. Explain factors an organization should consider when choosing between a paid loss and an incurred loss retrospective rating plan. (pp. 6.16–6.17)

Application Question

3-4. Parne Manufacturing (Parne) is trying to convince its insurer to provide it with a retrospective rating plan on a paid loss basis rather than on an incurred loss basis. Explain why Parne's insurer may be reluctant to do so.

Educational Objective 4
Describe the administration of retrospective rating plans.

Review Questions

4-1. Identify the administrative duties performed by the following entities under a retrospective rating plan: (p. 6.17)

   a. The insurer

   b. The insured

4-2. Explain why many insurers using a paid loss retrospective rating plan require the insured organization to provide collateral. (p. 6.17)

4-3. Identify the financial accounting issues an insured organization considers when using a retrospective rating plan. (p. 6.18)

Application Question

4-4. At the end of its policy year, an organization with a paid loss retrospective rating plan has $75,000 in paid losses and $450,000 in incurred losses. Based on its incurred losses, its retrospective rating premium is $550,000.

For financial accounting purposes, identify what the organization should use for its expense figure on its income statement at the end of the policy period.

Educational Objective 5
Describe the advantages and disadvantages of retrospective rating plans.

Review Questions

5-1. Identify two advantages of a retrospective rating plan over a guaranteed-cost insurance plan. (pp. 6.19–6.20)

5-2. Identify three possible disadvantages of a retrospective rating plan compared with a guaranteed-cost plan. (p. 6.20)

5-3. Identify a potential objection to the insurer's premium adjustment process under retrospective rating plans. (p. 6.20)

Application Question

5-4. Metal Etching Company's (MEC) risk management professional believes that MEC's workers' compensation losses will be minimal in the future because its new manufacturing process uses microbes to engrave metal instead of acid. Consequently, MEC's risk management professional has proposed purchasing a retrospective rating plan with low minimum premiums, high maximum premiums, and no loss limitation. What is the worst-case scenario under the proposed retrospective rating plan?

Educational Objective 6

Given a case, justify a retrospective rating plan that can meet an organization's risk financing needs.

Application Question

6-1. Complete the table on page 6.14 using the following data about Commercial Contractor's retrospective rating plan:

All years:
- Lines of insurance included: workers' compensation and general liability
- No loss limitation
- Minimum premium is 60 percent of standard premium
- Maximum premium is 120 percent of standard premium
- Basic premium is 25 percent of standard premium
- Tax rate is 4 percent

Years 1-2:
- Incurred loss retrospective rating plan
- Deposit premium equal to standard premium

Years 3-5:
- Paid loss retrospective rating plan
- Deposit premium equal to basic premium

Evaluate the effectiveness of Commercial Contractor's retrospective rating plan.

Year	Standard Premium	Deposit Premium	Basic Premium	Losses	Loss Conversion Factor	Adjusted Losses	Tax Multiplier	Retrospective Premium	Minimum Premium	Maximum Premium
1	$510,000			$240,000	1.10		1.04			
2	$545,000			$210,000	1.10		1.04			
3	$578,000			$301,000	1.11		1.04			
4	$601,000			$440,000	1.11		1.04			
5	$659,000			$400,000	1.20		1.04			

Answers to Assignment 6 Questions

NOTE: These answers are provided to give students a basic understanding of acceptable types of responses. They often are not the only valid answers and are not intended to provide an exhaustive response to the questions.

Educational Objective 1

1-1. A retrospective rating plan is considered a hybrid risk financing plan because it contains elements of both retention and transfer. It is a risk retention plan because the insured organization is paying for losses through the retrospective rating plan premium. It is a transfer plan because the insurer assumes the insured's losses above a specified monetary limit.

1-2. A retrospective rating plan encourages an insured organization to control losses because the retrospective premium reflects losses incurred during the policy period. The insured is rewarded through lower premiums to the extent that it controls losses.

1-3. Retrospective rating plans are commonly used to finance low- to medium-severity losses arising from liability loss exposures covered by workers' compensation, auto liability, and general liability insurance policies.

1-4. The premium under a guaranteed-cost insurance plan does not vary with the insured's losses that occur during the policy period. Under a retrospective rating plan, a premium deposit is paid at the beginning of the policy period and the insurer adjusts the premium upward or downward after the end of the policy period based directly on a portion of covered losses the insured organization incurs.

1-5. The following retrospective rating design factors affect the loss amounts paid by an insurer:
   a. Maximum premium—limits the premium amount an insured organization is required to pay regardless of the amount of incurred losses
   b. Minimum premium—establishes a minimum amount the insured organization is required to pay regardless of the amount of incurred losses
   c. Loss limit—caps the insured's losses used in calculating the retrospectively rated premium by using a loss limit for each individual or occurrence

1-6. Costs other than retained losses that are included in the premium under a retrospective rating plan are insurance charges. This component includes the insurer's overhead and profits, residual market loadings, and premium taxes.

1-7. LM's risk management professional explains to LM's CFO that an experience-rated guaranteed-cost insurance plan bases the current policy premium on past policy periods, whereas a retrospective rating plan bases the current policy premium on current year losses. Past losses are not completely ignored in retrospective rating plan premium; however, loss experience is less important relative to current losses.

Educational Objective 2

2-1. The following formula is used to calculate retrospective rating insurance premium:

Retrospective rating plan premium = (Basic premium + Converted losses + Excess loss premium) × Tax multiplier.

2-2. The following are the components of the retrospective rating insurance premium formula:
   a. Standard premium—manual premium multiplied by an experience modification factor
   b. Basic premium—includes insurer acquisition expenses, administrative costs, overhead, profit, and the insurance charge, which is expressed as a percentage of the insured organization's standard premium
   c. Converted losses—the product of incurred losses and an applicable loss conversion factor, which reflects allocated loss adjustment expenses
   d. Excess loss premium—the product of the standard premium and the excess loss premium factor, which compensates the insurer for the risk that an individual loss will exceed the loss limit
   e. Tax multiplier—a factor that covers the insurer's cost for state premium taxes, license fees, insurance organization assessments, and residual market loadings

2-3. A high loss conversion factor implies that the insurer expects that the losses will be costly to settle.

2-4. Calculations for XYZ's retrospective rating plan are as follows:
   a. XYZ's basic premium: Standard premium × Basic premium percentage
   $$\$500,000 \times 20\% = \$100,000.$$
   b. XYZ's excess loss premium: Standard premium × Excess loss premium factor percentage
   $$\$500,000 \times 5\% = \$25,000.$$
   c. XYZ's maximum premium: Standard premium × Maximum premium percentage
   $$\$500,000 \times 150\% = \$750,000.$$
   d. XYZ's minimum premium: Standard premium × Minimum premium percentage
   $$\$500,000 \times 40\% = \$200,000.$$

Educational Objective 3

3-1. An incurred loss retrospective rating plan differs from a paid loss retrospective rating plan because, under an incurred loss retrospective rating plan, the insured organization pays a deposit premium during the policy period and the premium is adjusted at the end of the policy period based on the insured organization's actual incurred losses. Under a paid loss retrospective rating plan, the insured organization pays a deposit premium at the beginning of the policy period and reimburses the insurer for its losses as the insurer pays for them.

3-2. Under an incurred loss retrospective rating plan, the insured organization does not receive the cash flow available on its loss reserves. The cash flow is held by the insurer. Under a paid loss plan, the insured organization benefits from cash flow available on the funds it retains rather than paying them to the insurer.

3-3. An organization should consider the following factors when choosing between a paid loss and an incurred loss retrospective rating plan:
   - The relationship between the amount that the insurer adds to the basic premium and the value of the cash flow benefit
   - The additional administrative tasks associated with a paid loss retrospective plan

3-4. Parne's insurer may be reluctant to provide a paid loss retrospective rating plan because (1) the insurer loses the cash flow that is available with an incurred loss retrospective rating plan, and (2) the insurer must bill Parne whenever it pays a loss, as well as verify the collateral used to secure the relationship.

Educational Objective 4

4-1. Entities perform the following administrative duties under a retrospective rating plan:
   a. Insurer—adjusting losses, making necessary filings with the state regulatory authorities, and paying applicable premium taxes and residual market loadings
   b. Insured—making premium payments and arranging for any required security collateral

4-2. Many insurers using a paid loss retrospective rating plan require the insured organization to provide collateral to guarantee that future premium adjustments will be paid.

4-3. An insured organization considers the following financial accounting issues when using a retrospective rating plan:
   - Future premium payments should be posted as a liability on the insured's balance sheet and as an expense on its income statement.
   - Additional premium for incurred but not retained losses should be posted as a liability on the insured's balance sheet and as an expense on its income statement.

4-4. For financial accounting purposes, the organization should use $550,000 for its expense figure on its income statement at the end of the policy period.

Educational Objective 5

5-1. Two advantages of a retrospective rating plan over a guaranteed-cost insurance plan are (1) its long-run cost tends to be lower than the cost of transfer and (2) it encourages risk control because of the direct link between losses and premium.

5-2. Possible disadvantages of a retrospective rating plan compared with a guaranteed-cost plan are:
   - If not properly designed, a retrospective rating plan can make financial planning difficult for the insured organization.
   - The insured organization could set unrealistically high reserves for the retained portion of losses, resulting in a loss of cash flow.
   - The losses ultimately retained by the insured are initially paid to the insurer and may result in premium tax and residual market loading expenses.

5-3. A potential objection to the insurer's premium adjustment process under retrospective rating plans is that an insurer may not adjust losses when it knows the insured organization is retaining them, resulting in loss payments that are higher than necessary.

5-4. In a worst-case scenario, MEC's risk management professional may be wrong about MEC's future losses. Consequently, MEC could incur losses equal to or greater than those incurred in the past. With no loss limitation and a high maximum premium, MEC's retrospective rating premium could be substantially larger than expected.

Educational Objective 6

6-1. Commercial Contractor's retrospective rating plan may be evaluated as follows:

Year	Standard Premium	Deposit Premium	Basic Premium	Losses	Loss Conversion Factor	Adjusted Losses	Tax Multiplier	Retrospective Premium	Minimum Premium	Maximum Premium	Retro Prem.> Standard Premium?
1	$510,000	$510,000	$127,500	$240,000	1.10	$264,000	1.04	$407,160	$306,000	$612,000	$102,840
2	$545,000	$545,000	$136,250	$210,000	1.10	$231,000	1.04	$381,940	$327,000	$654,000	$163,060
3	$578,000	$144,500	$144,500	$301,000	1.11	$344,110	1.04	$508,154	$346,800	$693,600	$ 69,846
4	$601,000	$150,250	$150,250	$440,000	1.11	$488,400	1.04	$664,196	$360,600	$721,200	$ −63,196
5	$659,000	$164,750	$164,750	$400,000	1.20	$480,000	1.04	$670,540	$395,400	$790,800	$ −11,540
Total Premium Savings											$ 261,010

Year 1 – [$127,500 + ($240,000 × 1.10)] × 1.04 = $407,160.
Year 2 – [$136,250 + ($210,000 × 1.10)] × 1.04 = $381,940.
Year 3 – [$144,500 + ($310,000 × 1.11)] × 1.04 = $508,154.
Year 4 – [$150,250 + ($440,000 × 1.11)] × 1.04 = $664,196.
Year 5 – [$164,750 + ($400,000 × 1.20)] × 1.04 = $670,540.

Over the past five years, Commercial Contractor has paid $261,010 less under its retrospective rating plan than it would have paid under a guaranteed-cost insurance plan.

Direct Your Learning

Reinsurance and Its Importance to a Risk Financing Program

Educational Objectives

After learning the content of this assignment, you should be able to:

1. Describe the purpose of reinsurance.
2. Describe the six functions of reinsurance.
3. Describe treaty reinsurance and facultative reinsurance.
4. Describe the three sources of reinsurance.
5. Describe the following types of pro rata reinsurance and their uses:
   - Quota share reinsurance
   - Surplus share reinsurance
6. Given a case, determine how the primary insurer and the reinsurer would share the amount of insurance, the premium, and covered losses under quota share and surplus share treaties.
7. Describe the following types of excess of loss reinsurance:
   - Per risk excess of loss reinsurance
   - Catastrophe excess of loss reinsurance
   - Per policy excess of loss reinsurance
   - Per occurrence excess of loss reinsurance
   - Aggregate excess of loss reinsurance
8. Given a case, determine how the primary insurer and the reinsurer would share losses under per risk excess of loss, catastrophe excess of loss, per policy excess of loss, per occurrence excess of loss, and aggregate excess of loss treaties.
9. Describe the characteristics of finite risk reinsurance.
10. Explain the reinsurance concerns of risk management professionals.
11. Given a case, identify how an organization may benefit from its insurer's use of reinsurance or the use of reinsurance with its captive insurer.
12. Define or describe each of the Key Words and Phrases for this assignment.

Study Materials

Required Reading:
- Risk Financing
  - Chapter 7

Study Aids:
- SMART Online Practice Exam
- SMART Study Aids
  - Review Notes and Flash Cards—Assignment 7

Outline

- **Reinsurance Defined**
- **Reinsurance Functions**
    - A. Increase Large Line Capacity
    - B. Provide Catastrophe Protection
    - C. Stabilize Loss Experience
    - D. Provide Surplus Relief
    - E. Facilitate Withdrawal From a Market Segment
    - F. Provide Underwriting Guidance
- **Reinsurance Transactions**
    - A. Treaty Reinsurance
    - B. Facultative Reinsurance
- **Reinsurance Sources**
    - A. Professional Reinsurers
    - B. Reinsurance Departments of Primary Insurers
    - C. Reinsurance Pools, Syndicates, and Associations
- **Reinsurance Types**
    - A. Pro Rata Reinsurance
        1. Quota Share Reinsurance
        2. Surplus Share Reinsurance
    - B. Excess of Loss Reinsurance
        1. Per Risk Excess of Loss Reinsurance
        2. Catastrophe Excess of Loss Reinsurance
        3. Per Policy Excess of Loss Reinsurance
        4. Per Occurrence Excess of Loss Reinsurance
        5. Aggregate Excess of Loss Reinsurance
    - C. Finite Risk Reinsurance
- **Reinsurance Concerns of Risk Management Professionals**
    - A. Portfolio Reinsurance Arrangements
    - B. Cut-Through Endorsements
    - C. Reinsurance Through a Subsidiary
    - D. Reinsuring a Pool
    - E. Cooperation Between Insurers and Reinsurers to Provide Capacity
- **Reinsurance Case Studies**
    - A. Property Management Company
    - B. Amusement Park Company
    - C. Transit Company
- **Summary**

 Set aside a specific, realistic amount of time to study every day.

For each assignment, you should define or describe each of the Key Words and Phrases and answer each of the Review and Application Questions.

> ### Educational Objective 1
> Describe the purpose of reinsurance.

Key Words and Phrases

Reinsurance (p. 7.3)

Reinsurer (p. 7.3)

Reinsurance premium (p. 7.3)

Primary insurer (p. 7.3)

Insurance risk (p. 7.3)

Retrocession (p. 7.4)

Review Questions

1-1. Identify the parties involved in a reinsurance agreement. (p. 7.3)

1-2. List terms that may be used to refer to the primary insurer in a reinsurance agreement. (p. 7.3)

1-3. Describe the conditions usually included in a reinsurance agreement. (pp. 7.3–7.4)

Application Question

1-4. Shopping Mall's (SM) risk management professional learns through her insurance broker that SM's insurer is reinsuring a significant share of its property loss exposure. SM's risk management professional understands that SM must now deal with its insurer and this reinsurer if a loss occurs. Explain how the purchase of reinsurance affects SM's relationship with its insurer, if at all.

> **Educational Objective 2**
> Describe the six functions of reinsurance.

Key Words and Phrases

Line (p. 7.4)

Large line capacity (p. 7.5)

Policyholders' surplus (p. 7.7)

Net written premiums (p. 7.7)

Capacity ratio (p. 7.7)

Ceding commission (p. 7.7)

Surplus relief (p. 7.7)

Portfolio reinsurance (p. 7.8)

Novation (p. 7.8)

Review Questions

2-1. List the six principal functions of reinsurance. (p. 7.4)

2-2. Describe factors that influence the maximum amount of insurance or limit of liability that an insurer will accept on a single loss exposure. (p. 7.4)

2-3. Describe the possible financial consequences volatile loss experience may have on a primary insurer. (p. 7.5)

2-4. Describe the ways in which reinsurance can stabilize the loss experience of primary insurers. (p. 7.5)

2-5. Identify three reasons why a primary insurer may choose to withdrawal from a market segment. (p. 7.8)

2-6. Identify options available to a primary insurer when it decides to withdrawal from a market segment. (p. 7.8)

2-7. Contrast portfolio reinsurance and novation. (p. 7.8)

Application Question

2-8. ABC Insurance Company (ABC) has net written premiums of $440 million, assets of $800 million, and liabilities of $400 million. What is ABC's capacity ratio?

Educational Objective 3

Describe treaty reinsurance and facultative reinsurance.

Key Words and Phrases

Treaty reinsurance (p. 7.9)

Facultative reinsurance (p. 7.9)

Adverse selection (p. 7.10)

Facultative certificate of reinsurance (p. 7.10)

Review Questions

3-1. Describe two types of reinsurance transactions. (p. 7.9)

3-2. Explain why treaty reinsurance is sometimes called obligatory reinsurance. (p. 7.9)

3-3. Explain why facultative reinsurance is sometimes called nonobligatory reinsurance. (p. 7.9)

3-4. Identify four functions that facultative reinsurance serves. (pp. 7.10–7.11)

Application Question

3-5. For each of the following cases, identify the type of reinsurance (facultative or treaty) that would be most appropriate:

 a. Lawton Insurance has been offered the opportunity to insure the builder's risk coverage on what will be the largest shopping mall in the United States.

 b. Spring Insurance is expanding its market by licensing agents in California, Oregon, and Washington for homeowners and personal auto insurance.

Educational Objective 4
Describe the three sources of reinsurance.

Key Words and Phrases
Professional reinsurer (p. 7.11)

Direct writing reinsurer (p. 7.11)

Reinsurance intermediary (p. 7.12)

Reinsurance pools, syndicates, and associations (p. 7.13)

Review Questions

4-1. Identify three sources for purchasing reinsurance. (p. 7.11)

4-2. Describe the marketing relationship of the following professional reinsurers with primary insurers: (pp. 7.11–7.12)

   a. Direct writing reinsurer

b. Reinsurance intermediary

4-3. Describe issues that professional reinsurers and primary insurers should consider before entering a reinsurance agreement. (pp. 7.12–7.13)

Application Question

4-4. For each of the following cases, identify the most likely source of reinsurance for the primary insurer.

a. XYZ Insurance has had problems in the past with complex reinsurance programs involving many reinsurers from all over the world.

b. Danford Insurance specializes in insuring oil refineries.

c. Atwell Insurance sells property insurance for oceanfront homes and businesses on both the east coast and the west coast of the United States.

> **Educational Objective 5**
> Describe the following types of pro rata reinsurance and their uses:
> - Quota share reinsurance
> - Surplus share reinsurance

Key Words and Phrases

Pro rata reinsurance (p. 7.14)

Loss adjustment expenses (p. 7.14)

Flat commission (p. 7.15)

Profit-sharing commission (p. 7.15)

Sliding scale commission (in reinsurance) (p. 7.15)

Quota share reinsurance (p. 7.15)

Loss ratio (p. 7.15)

Variable quota share treaty (p. 7.17)

Surplus share reinsurance (p. 7.17)

Bordereau (p. 7.19)

Line guide (p. 7.20)

Review Questions

5-1. Describe the two types of pro rata reinsurance. (pp. 7.14–7.15)

5-2. Describe the basis on which policy premiums and losses are shared between the primary insurer and the reinsurer in a surplus share treaty. (p. 7.17)

5-3. Explain how primary insurer underwriters establish the retention for each loss exposure subject to a surplus share treaty. (pp. 7.19–7.20)

Application Question

5-4. A primary insurer has a five-line surplus share treaty with a $3 million limit. For a specific loss exposure with coverage limit needs of $2.5 million, the primary insurer's line guide permits a $500,000 line. Calculate the percentage that will be used to share premiums and losses between the primary insurer and the reinsurer.

Educational Objective 6

Given a case, determine how the primary insurer and the reinsurer would share the amount of insurance, the premium, and covered losses under quota share and surplus share treaties.

Application Question

6-1. Callaway Insurance Company (Callaway) has a 70 percent quota share treaty with a reinsurance limit of $750,000. Show how amounts of insurance, policy premiums and losses will be shared in the following scenarios:

a. Policy A has a $250,000 amount of insurance, a policy premium of $20,000, and a $100,000 loss.

Policy A	Callaway	Reinsurer
Amounts of insurance	$	$
Policy premiums	$	$
Losses	$	$

b. Policy B has a $500,000 amount of insurance, a policy premium of $40,000 and a $250,000 loss.

Policy B	Callaway	Reinsurer
Amounts of insurance	$	$
Policy premiums	$	$
Losses	$	$

Educational Objective 7

Describe the following types of excess of loss reinsurance:

- Per risk excess of loss reinsurance
- Catastrophe excess of loss reinsurance
- Per policy excess of loss reinsurance
- Per occurrence excess of loss reinsurance
- Aggregate excess of loss reinsurance

Key Words and Phrases

Excess of loss reinsurance (p. 7.20)

Attachment point (p. 7.20)

Subject premium (p. 7.21)

Working cover (p. 7.21)

Co-participation provision (p. 7.22)

Per risk excess of loss reinsurance (p. 7.23)

Catastrophe excess of loss reinsurance (p. 7.24)

Loss occurrence clause (p. 7.24)

Per policy excess of loss reinsurance (p. 7.26)

Per occurrence excess of loss reinsurance (p. 7.27)

Aggregate excess of loss reinsurance (p. 7.28)

Review Questions

7-1. Describe the five types of excess of loss reinsurance. (pp. 7.20–7.28)

7-2. Describe the importance of the attachment point in excess of loss reinsurance. (pp. 7.20–7.21)

7-3. Identify two factors that affect the extent of a reinsurer's obligation to indemnify a primary insurer in excess of loss reinsurance. (p. 7.21)

7-4. Describe how a reinsurance agreement with a low attachment point benefits the primary insurer. (p. 7.22)

7-5. Identify two common approaches to handling loss adjustment expenses. (pp. 7.22–7.23)

7-6. Identify how the scope of a catastrophic occurrence is defined in a catastrophic excess of loss reinsurance agreement. (p. 7.24)

Application Question

7-7. Using the table, determine which layers, and to what extent, each of the following losses would fall:

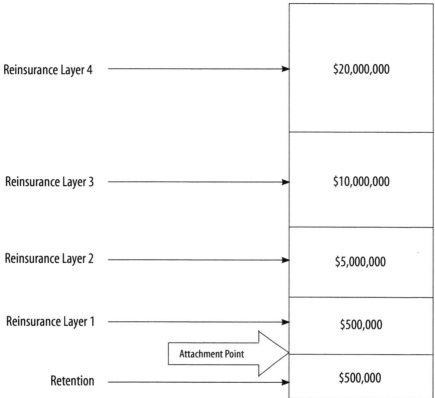

a. $100,000

b. $750,000

c. $15,000,000

d. $25,000,000

Educational Objective 8

Given a case, determine how the primary insurer and the reinsurer would share losses under per risk excess of loss, catastrophe excess of loss, per policy excess of loss, per occurrence excess of loss, and aggregate excess of loss treaties.

Application Question

8-1. An insurer purchases a $750,000 xs $250,000 excess of loss treaty with a 10 percent co-participation provision. What amounts would (1) the primary insurer and (2) the reinsurer pay for the following losses?

   a. $200,000

   b. $500,000

   c. $1,000,000

   d. $1,250,000

Educational Objective 9

Describe the characteristics of finite risk reinsurance.

Key Word or Phrase

Finite risk reinsurance (p. 7.29)

Review Questions

9-1. Explain why finite risk reinsurance is sometimes called financial reinsurance. (p. 7.29)

9-2. Identify the characteristics of finite risk reinsurance. (p. 7.29)

9-3. Identify the types of loss exposures effectively handled by finite risk reinsurance. (p. 7.29)

Application Question

9-4. Atwell Insurance (Atwell) purchases a five-year finite risk reinsurance plan to cover its catastrophe exposure in southern Florida. The agreement has a $10 million nonreinstateable limit. The annual premium is $1.75 million, payable even if the limit of the agreement has been exhausted. At the end of the five-year term, the finite risk reinsurer will pay $5 million in profit sharing to Atwell if no losses occur.

   a. Explain the extent of the insurance risk transferred to the reinsurer.

   b. Explain how this agreement might allow Atwell to create a catastrophe fund.

Educational Objective 10
Explain the reinsurance concerns of risk management professionals.

Key Word or Phrase
Cut-through endorsement (p. 7.31)

Review Questions

10-1. Identify situations in which a risk management professional would deal directly with a reinsurer. (p. 7.30)

10-2. Explain why a risk management professional whose insurance plan has been reinsured through a portfolio reinsurance arrangement should be aware of details of the transaction. (p. 7.30)

10-3. Explain how adding a cut-through endorsement to a reinsurance agreement is advantageous to the insured. (pp. 7.31–7.32)

10-4. Explain what factors a risk management professional should consider when reinsuring risk through a pool. (p. 7.32)

Application Question

10-5. Telephone Service Company (TSC) forms an insurance subsidiary (captive) to handle its property and liability insurance needs. Explain the role, if any, that reinsurance may have in TSC's subsidiary's operation. (pp. 7.4–7.5, 7.32)

Educational Objective 11

Given a case, identify how an organization may benefit from its insurer's use of reinsurance or the use of reinsurance with its captive insurer.

Application Question

11-1. Seaside Resort Construction Company (SRCC) has trouble placing its large insurance program at a reasonable price each year. Explain how the price of reinsurance affects SRCC's insurance program.

Answers to Assignment 7 Questions

NOTE: These answers are provided to give students a basic understanding of acceptable types of responses. They often are not the only valid answers and are not intended to provide an exhaustive response to the questions.

Educational Objective 1

1-1. Parties involved in a reinsurance agreement include the following:
- Reinsurer—insurer that assumes all or part of the insurance risk
- Primary insurer—insurer that transfers or cedes all or part of the insurance risk

1-2. Terms used to refer to the primary insurer in a reinsurance agreement include the ceding company, the cedent, the reinsured, or the direct insurer.

1-3. The following conditions are usually contained in a reinsurance agreement:
- Usually requires the primary insurer to keep part of its original liability
- Does not alter the terms of the underlying (original) insurance policies or the primary insurer's obligations to honor them
- Specifies the terms under which the reinsurance is provided
- Identifies the policy, group of policies, or other categories of insurance that are included in the agreement

1-4. The reinsurance agreement does not alter the terms of the underlying (original) insurance policies or the primary insurer's obligations to honor them.

Educational Objective 2

2-1. The following are the principal functions of reinsurance:
  (1) Increase large line capacity
  (2) Provide catastrophe protection
  (3) Stabilize loss experience
  (4) Provide surplus relief
  (5) Facilitate withdrawal from a market segment
  (6) Provide underwriting guidance

2-2. The following factors influence the maximum amount of insurance or limit of liability that an insurer will accept on a single loss exposure:
- Maximum amount of insurance or limit of liability allowed by insurance regulations. Regulations prohibit an insurer from retaining more than 10 percent of its policyholders' surplus on any one loss exposure.
- The size of a potential loss or losses that an insurer can safely retain without impairing earnings or policyholders' surplus.
- Specific characteristics of a particular loss exposure.
- Amount, types, and cost of available reinsurance.

2-3. Volatile loss experience may have the following financial consequences for a primary insurer:
- Affect the stock value of a publicly traded insurer
- Alter an insurer's financial rating by independent rating agencies
- Cause abrupt changes in the approaches the insurer takes in managing the underwriting, claim, and marketing departments
- Undermine the confidence of the sales force
- Possibly lead to insolvency

2-4. Reinsurance can stabilize a primary insurer's loss experience by doing any or all of the following:
- Limit its liability for a single loss exposure
- Limit its liability for several loss exposures affected by a common event
- Limit its liability for loss exposures that aggregate claims over time

2-5. A primary insurer may choose to withdrawal from a market segment that is unprofitable, undesirable, or does not fit into its strategic plan.

2-6. Options a primary insurer may have when it decides to withdrawal from a market include:
- To stop selling new insurance policies and continue in-force insurance until all policies expire
- To cancel all policies and refund the unearned premiums to insureds
- To withdrawal from the market segment by purchasing portfolio reinsurance

2-7. Portfolio reinsurance and novation differ in the following way:

In a portfolio reinsurance transaction, the primary insurer accepts all of the liability for certain loss exposures covered under the primary insurer's policies, however must continue to fulfill its obligations to its insureds.

In a novation, the substitute insurer assumes the direct obligations to insureds covered by the underlying insurance.

2-8. ABC's capacity ratio is 1.1 to 1 and is calculated as follows:

Policyholder's surplus = Assets − Liabilities
= $800 million − $400 million
= $400 million

Capacity ratio = Net written premiums ÷ Policyholders' surplus
= $440 million ÷ $400 million
= 1.1 or 1.1 to 1

Educational Objective 3

3-1. The following are two types of reinsurance transactions:
- Treaty—The agreement covers an entire class or portfolio of loss exposures and provides that the primary insurer's individual loss exposures that fall within the treaty are automatically reinsured.
- Facultative—The reinsurer underwrites each loss exposure separately.

3-2. Treaty reinsurance is sometimes called obligatory reinsurance because the reinsurance agreement covers an entire class or portfolio of loss exposures and loss exposures that fall within the treaty are automatically reinsured.

3-3. Facultative reinsurance is sometimes called nonobligatory reinsurance because the primary insurer chooses which loss exposures to submit to the reinsurer, and the reinsurer can accept or reject any loss exposures submitted.

3-4. Four functions that facultative reinsurance provides primary insurers are the following:
   (1) To provide large line capacity for loss exposures that exceed the limits of treaty reinsurance agreements
   (2) To reduce the primary insurer's exposure in a given geographic area
   (3) To insure a loss exposure with atypical hazard characteristics and thereby maintain the favorable loss experience of the primary insurer's treaty reinsurance and any associated profit-sharing arrangements
   (4) To insure particular classes of loss exposures that are excluded under treaty reinsurance

3-5. The following would be appropriate types of reinsurance for each company:
   a. Lawton Insurance will need facultative reinsurance to provide the capacity to insure this loss exposure because the suggested size of this loss exposure will likely exceed the large line capacity of its existing treaties.
   b. Spring Insurance will need treaty reinsurance to insure the many loss exposures and obtain automatic acceptance by its reinsurers. Spring needs a treaty because of the volume of loss exposures it can expect in this new market.

Educational Objective 4

4-1. Three sources for purchasing reinsurance are professional reinsurers; reinsurance departments of primary insurers; and reinsurance pools, syndicates, and associations.

4-2. The marketing relationship of professional reinsurers with primary insurers is as follows:
   a. Direct writing reinsurer—Employees deal directly with primary insurers and also solicit reinsurance business through reinsurance intermediaries.
   b. Reinsurance intermediary—The broker represents the primary insurer and negotiates reinsurance agreements between the primary insurer and one or more reinsurers.

4-3. Before entering into a reinsurance agreement, the following issues should be considered:
   - Professional reinsurers should gather information about the primary insurer's financial strength by analyzing financial statements, by using information developed by a financial rating service, or from state insurance department bulletins. Reinsurers should also consider the primary insurer's experience, reputation, and management.
   - Primary insurers should evaluate the reinsurer's claim paying ability, reputation, management competence.

4-4. For the stated cases, the following are the most likely sources of reinsurance for the primary insurer:
   a. XYZ Insurance may be more satisfied with a reinsurance program provided by a single direct writing reinsurer who will be able to provide all its reinsurance needs, rather than a group of reinsurers.

b. Danford Insurance's specialization in oil refinery loss exposures indicates its need to obtain reinsurance from a diverse group of reinsurers assembled by a reinsurance intermediary.

c. Atwell Insurance has a significant catastrophe exposure to wind. Reinsurance intermediaries are often best positioned to structure large catastrophe programs.

Educational Objective 5

5-1. The following are two types of pro rata reinsurance:
- Quota share reinsurance—The primary insurer and the reinsurer share the amounts of insurance, policy premiums, and losses using a fixed percentage.
- Surplus share reinsurance—The policies covered are those whose amount of insurance exceeds a stipulated dollar amount, or line.

5-2. In a surplus share treaty, policy premiums and losses are shared proportionately between the primary insurer and the reinsurer on a percentage basis. The primary insurer's share of the policy premiums and losses is that proportion that the line bears to the total amount of insurance. The reinsurer's share is that proportion that the amount ceded bears to the total.

5-3. Primary insurer underwriters establish the retention for each loss exposure subject to a surplus share treaty through a line guide. The line guide provides the minimum and maximum line that the primary insurer can retain on a loss exposure.

5-4. The primary insurer will need to retain 20 percent of all losses and policy premiums while ceding 80 percent of all losses and policy premiums. The cession percentage was determined by dividing $500,000 by $2,500,000.

Educational Objective 6

6-1. Amounts of insurance, policy premiums and losses for Callaway will be shared in the following way:

a. Policy A with $250,000 amount of insurance, a policy premium of $20,000, and a $100,000 loss:

Policy A	Callaway	Reinsurer
Amounts of insurance	$75,000 (30 percent)	$175,000 (70 percent)
Policy premiums	$6,000 (30 percent)	$14,000 (70 percent)
Losses	$30,000 (30 percent)	$70,000 (70 percent)

b. Policy B with $500,000 amount of insurance, a policy premium of $40,000 and a $250,000 loss:

Policy B	Callaway	Reinsurer
Amounts of insurance	$150,000 (30 percent)	$350,000 (70 percent)
Policy premiums	$12,000 (30 percent)	$28,000 (70 percent)
Losses	$75,000 (30 percent)	$175,000 (70 percent)

Educational Objective 7

7-1. The following are the five types of excess of loss reinsurance:
(1) Per risk excess of loss—typically used for property loss exposures and applies separately to each loss occurring to each risk
(2) Catastrophe excess of loss—typically used for property loss exposures to protect the primary insurer from an accumulation of retained losses that arise from a single catastrophic event
(3) Per policy excess of loss—typically used for liability loss exposures and applies the attachment point and the reinsurance limit separately to each insurance policy issued by the primary insurer regardless of the number of losses occurring under each policy
(4) Per occurrence excess of loss—typically used for liability loss exposures and applies the attachment point and the reinsurance limit to the total losses arising from a single event affecting one or more of the primary insurer's policies
(5) Aggregate excess of loss—used for both property and liability loss exposures and covers aggregated losses that exceed the attachment point and that occur over a stated period

7-2. The importance of the attachment point in excess of loss reinsurance is that it represents the point at which the loss amount exceeds a specified dollar amount and the point at which the reinsurer responds to a loss. The primary insurer fully retains losses that are less than the attachment point and the reinsurer sometimes requires the primary insurer to also retain responsibility for a percentage that exceed the attachment point.

7-3. Two factors that affect the extent of a reinsurer's obligation to indemnify a primary insurer in excess of loss reinsurance are (1) the amount of the loss and (2) the layer of coverage that the reinsurer provides.

7-4. A reinsurance agreement with a low attachment point may anticipate that the primary insurer's volume of losses will be significant. The low attachment point benefits the primary insurer by enabling it to spread its losses over several years.

7-5. The following are two common approaches to handling loss adjustment expenses:
(1) Pro rata in addition—Loss adjustment expenses are prorated between the primary insurer and the reinsurer based on the same percentage share that each is responsible for the loss.
(2) Included in the limit—Loss adjustment expenses are added to the amount of the loss when applying the attachment point of the excess of loss reinsurance agreement.

7-6. The scope of a catastrophic occurrence is defined in a catastrophic excess of loss reinsurance agreement through a loss occurrence clause. This clause specifies a period, in hours, during which the primary insurer's losses arising out of the same catastrophic occurrence can be aggregated and applied to the attachment point and reinsurance limits.

7-7. (a) The primary insurer would retain the full amount $100,000.
(b) The primary insurer would retain $500,000, and $250,000 would be paid by the first reinsurance layer.
(c) The primary insurer would retain $500,000. The first reinsurance layer would pay $500,000, the second reinsurance layer would pay $5,000,000, and the third reinsurance layer would pay $9,000,000.

(d) The primary insurer would retain $500,000. The first reinsurance layer would pay $500,000, the second reinsurance layer would pay $5,000,000, the third reinsurance layer would pay $10,000,000, and the fourth reinsurance layer would pay $9,000,000.

Educational Objective 8

8-1. With an excess of loss treaty with a 10 percent co-participation provision, the primary insurer and the reinsurer would pay the following amounts:
   a. $200,000 loss:
      - Primary insurer would pay $200,000—The amount of the loss is within the retention.
      - Reinsurer would pay $0—The amount of loss is within the retention.
   b. $500,000 loss:
      - Primary insurer would pay $275,000—The amount of the retention ($250,000) plus 10 percent of the amount in excess of the retention ($25,000).
      - Reinsurer would pay $225,000—The amount of loss ($500,000) less the $275,000 payable by the primary insurer.
   c. $1,000,000 loss:
      - Primary insurer would pay $325,000—The amount of the retention ($250,000) plus 10 percent of the amount in excess of the retention ($75,000).
      - Reinsurer would pay $675,000—The amount of loss ($1,000,000) less the $325,000 payable by the primary insurer.
   d. $1,250,000 loss:
      - Primary insurer would pay $575,000—The amount of the retention ($250,000) plus 10 percent of the amount in excess of the retention up to the treaty limit ($75,000) plus the amount that exceeds the reinsurer's limit ($250,000).
      - Reinsurer would pay $675,000—The amount of loss below the treaty limit that is not payable by the primary insurer.

Educational Objective 9

9-1. Finite risk reinsurance is sometimes called financial reinsurance because this type of reinsurance transfers a limited amount of risk to the reinsurer with the objective of improving the primary insurer's financial result.

9-2. The characteristics of finite risk reinsurance include the following:
   - A limited transfer of insurance risk to the reinsurer
   - Anticipated investment income is expressly acknowledged as an underwriting component
   - Used with a combination of traditionally insurable and traditionally uninsurable loss exposures
   - Usually provided for a multi-year term
   - Reinsurer premium can be a substantial percentage of the reinsurance limit
   - Designed to cover high-severity losses

9-3. Finite risk reinsurance can effectively handle the following types of loss exposures:

- Insurable loss exposures, such as building loss due to explosion
- Traditionally uninsurable loss exposures, such as loss due to economic variables
- Extremely large and unusual loss exposures, such as catastrophic losses

9-4. The following are true regarding Atwell's five-year finite risk reinsurance agreement:

   a. Atwell is paying $8.75 million for $10 million in coverage. Ignoring investment income that the finite risk reinsurer earns on the reinsurance premium, the transferred insurance risk is $1.25 million

   b. If no losses occur, Atwell will have $5 million at the end of the five-year term. This amount can be used to pay future catastrophe losses.

Educational Objective 10

10-1. The following are situations in which a risk management professional would deal directly with a reinsurer:
   - A reinsurer takes the place of an insurer as a result of a portfolio reinsurance arrangement.
   - A reinsurer takes the place of an insurer through a cut-through endorsement added to an insurance policy.
   - An organization establishes a subsidiary that insures or reinsurers the organization's loss exposures.
   - An organization purchases reinsurance for a pool of which it is a member.
   - A reinsurer or several reinsurers team up with an insurer or several insurers to provide coverage.

10-2. A risk management professional whose insurance plan has been reinsured through a portfolio reinsurance arrangement should learn the details of the transaction in order to ascertain that coverage is maintained and that the reinsurer is at least as financially sound as the retiring insurer.

10-3. Adding a cut-through endorsement to a reinsurance agreement is advantageous to the insured in situations of reinsurer insolvency because it provides the insured with direct rights against the reinsurer, bypassing the primary insurer's insolvency proceedings.

10-4. Factors a risk management professional should consider when reinsuring risk through a pool are the pool's reinsurer's financial strength, integrity, and operating efficiency, which all affect the pool's reliability, and the solidarity and effectiveness of the organization's risk financing program.

10-5. Telephone Service Company benefits indirectly from reinsurance. Reinsurance allows TSC's insurer to insure properties with large values, particularly in wind-prone areas. Reinsurance also enables TSC's insurer to provide TSC with all its insurance needs instead of TSC's risk management professional having to gather participation from many insurers.

Educational Objective 11

11-1. Seaside Resort Construction Company needs large coverage limits in a part of the country that is subject to hurricanes. Consequently, SRCC's insurer's pricing must reflect the pricing (and availability) of its reinsurers.

Direct Your Learning

Captive Insurance Plans

Educational Objectives

After learning the content of this assignment, you should be able to:

1. Describe the purpose and characteristics of captive insurance plans.
2. Describe the types of captive insurance plans available.
3. Describe the advantages and disadvantages of using a captive insurance plan.
4. Explain how captive insurance plans operate.
5. Define or describe each of the Key Words and Phrases for this assignment.

Study Materials

Required Reading:
- Risk Financing
  - Chapter 8

Study Aids:
- SMART Online Practice Exam
- SMART Study Aids
  - Review Notes and Flash Cards—Assignment 8

Outline

- **Purpose and Characteristics of Captive Insurance Plans**
  A. Retaining and Transferring Losses
  B. Combining a Captive Insurance Plan With Transfer and Hybrid Risk Financing Plans
- **Types of Captive Insurance Plans**
  A. Single-Parent (or Pure) Captive
  B. Group Captive
  C. Risk Retention Group
  D. Agency Captive
  E. Rent-a-Captive
  F. Protected Cell Company
- **Advantages and Disadvantages of Using a Captive Insurance Plan**
  A. Advantages of Using a Captive Insurance Plan
    1. Reducing the Cost of Risk
    2. Benefiting From Cash Flow
    3. Obtaining Insurance Not Otherwise Available
    4. Having Direct Access to Reinsurers
    5. Negotiating With Insurers
    6. Centralizing Loss Retention
    7. Obtaining Potential Cash Flow Advantages on Income Taxes
    8. Controlling Losses
    9. Obtaining Rate Equity
  B. Disadvantages of Using a Captive Insurance Plan
    1. Capital and Start-Up Costs
    2. Sensitivity to Losses
    3. Pressure From Parent Company Management
    4. Premium Taxes and Residual Market Loadings
- **Operation of Captive Insurance Plans**
  A. Conducting a Feasibility Study
  B. Operating as a Reinsurer
  C. Operating as a Direct Writing Captive Insurer
  D. Selecting Coverages
  E. Setting Premiums
  F. Determining Domicile
  G. Dedicating Management Resources of Parent Organizations
  H. Administering the Plan
  I. Insuring Third-Party Business
  J. Understanding Financial Accounting Issues
- **Summary**

 Plan to take one week to complete each assignment in your course.

For each assignment, you should define or describe each of the Key Words and Phrases and answer each of the Review and Application Questions.

Educational Objective 1

Describe the purpose and characteristics of captive insurance plans.

Key Word or Phrase

Captive insurer (p. 8.3)

Review Questions

1-1. Describe the purpose of a captive insurance plan. (p. 8.3)

1-2. Identify actions a captive performs for its parent company. (p. 8.3)

1-3. List general characteristics of a common captive insurance plan. (p. 8.6)

Application Question

1-4. Barnley, Inc., is a manufacturer of lawnmowers. With spring mowing season rapidly approaching, Barnley's executive management group is eager to assure its board of directors that it has adequately covered the company's product liability exposures up to $20 million per occurrence. The executive group has asked its risk management professional to provide it with an illustration of the current coverage plan. The plan uses a captive insurer that issued a policy with a $1.5 million limit to Barnley. The captive policy includes a $500,000 retention and transfers the next $1 million in coverage to an excess of loss reinsurer. At the $1.5 million level, the company has transferred its exposure for the next $18.5 million to an insurer on a guaranteed-cost basis with an excess insurance policy. Illustrate these coverages in a manner similar to Exhibit 8-3 in the text.

Educational Objective 2
Describe the types of captive insurance plans available.

Key Words and Phrases
Single-parent, or pure, captive (p. 8.7)

Group captive (p. 8.7)

Association captive (p. 8.7)

Risk retention group (p. 8.7)

Agency captive (p. 8.8)

Rent-a-captive (p. 8.8)

Protected cell company (PCC) (p. 8.8)

Review Questions

2-1. Identify characteristics of the following types of captives: (p. 8.7)
   a. Single-parent captive

   b. Group captive

2-2. Explain the circumstances in which a single-parent captive is considered a hybrid risk financing plan. (p. 8.7)

2-3. Explain how an agent or broker can generate underwriting and investment income using a captive. (p. 8.8)

Application Question

2-4. Surewell is one of a few cookware manufacturers that uses a certain nonstick coating. The company is having difficulty finding affordable or available workers' compensation coverage, partially because of the hazardous processes it uses to produce the cookware. The company does not have the minimum required capital to establish its own captive. It wants to protect its capital by ensuring that any premiums it would pay to a captive insurer would not be affected by the losses of other insureds. If Surewell's risk management professional wants to be sure its premiums will be used only to pay for its own losses and not those of other insureds, which type of captive insurer should it use and why?

Educational Objective 3
Describe the advantages and disadvantages of using a captive insurance plan.

Key Words and Phrases
Risk shifting (p. 8.11)

Risk distribution (p. 8.11)

Brother-sister relationship (p. 8.12)

Third-party business (p. 8.12)

Review Questions

3-1. Identify ways a captive may help an organization reduce its cost of risk. (pp. 8.9–8.10)

3-2. Describe how having direct access to reinsurers may benefit a captive insurer. (p. 8.10)

3-3. Identify the two key factors the IRS uses to determine whether an insured's premiums paid to the captive insurer are tax-deductible. (p. 8.12)

3-4. Describe possible disadvantages of using a captive insurance plan. (pp. 8.13–8.15)

Application Question

3-5. An architectural firm is considering joining an association captive. However, its senior partners are reluctant to sever a long-standing relationship with the firm's insurance agent, who they believe has negotiated to the best of his abilities to obtain an acceptable rate from the firm's professional liability insurer. The managing partner has assumed the risk management responsibilities for the firm. What advantages can the managing partner point out to the senior partners that the firm may gain if it uses the existence of a captive insurer in its discussions with its commercial insurer?

Educational Objective 4
Explain how captive insurance plans operate.

Key Words and Phrases
Fronting company (p. 8.16)

Direct writing captive insurer (p. 8.18)

Review Questions

4-1. Describe how a risk management professional should conduct a captive insurance plan feasibility study. (pp. 8.15–8.16)

4-2. Explain why captive insurers use fronting companies. (p. 8.16)

4-3. Explain why a fronting company may require a letter of credit from the captive insurer. (p. 8.18)

4-4. Describe the premium arrangement between a parent and the captive insurer using the following bases: (p. 8.19)
   a. Guaranteed-cost basis

   b. Retrospectively rated basis

4-5. List the factors an organization should consider when evaluating the domicile of a captive. (p. 8.21)

Application Question

4-6. Assume KYZ Technology (KYZ) establishes a single-parent captive insurer and uses it to cover its automobile liability and general liability loss exposures up to a limit of $2 million per occurrence/accident. In order to comply with regulatory requirements, KYZ's captive reinsures a fronting company, which issues the $2 million limit policies to KYZ.

Assume the insurance arrangement between KYZ and the fronting company is an incurred loss retrospective rating plan with a loss limit of $250,000 per occurrence/accident. Therefore, KYZ, in effect, retains the first $250,000 of its own losses through the retrospective rating plan. KYZ's captive reinsures the fronting company on the same basis as the insurance between KYZ and the fronting company.

Assume KYZ's captive insurer purchases excess of loss reinsurance of $1 million excess of $1 million per occurrence/accident. (It does not purchase aggregate excess of loss reinsurance.) What is the risk of loss (on a net basis) assumed by KYZ's captive insurer?

Answers to Assignment 8 Questions

NOTE: These answers are provided to give students a basic understanding of acceptable types of responses. They often are not the only valid answers and are not intended to provide an exhaustive response to the questions.

Educational Objective 1

1-1. The purpose of a captive insurance plan is to provide insurance coverage to the parent in a manner that reduces the parent's cost of risk.

1-2. A captive collects premiums, issues policies, and pays covered losses for its parent company.

1-3. The following are general characteristics of a common captive insurer plan:
- Contains aspects of retention and transfer (hybrid plan)
- Covers low to medium loss severity
- Losses are funded
- Substantial administrative requirements

1-4. Barnley's coverages are illustrated as follows:

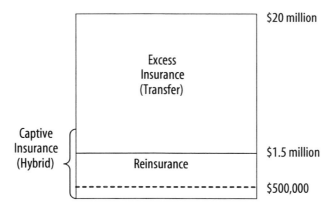

Educational Objective 2

2-1. Characteristics of captives include the following:
   a. Single-parent captive
   - Owned by one company
   - Requires an investment of capital and expenditures by its parent
   - Insures loss exposures that generate substantial premium revenues for the captive
   - Generally requires a minimum annual premium of $2 million

   b. Group captive
   - Owned by a group of companies
   - Insureds exercise a great deal of control over the management

2-2. A single-parent captive is considered a hybrid risk financing plan because it combines elements of retention and transfer. The captive covers its parent's losses and losses retained by the captive are retained by its parent.

2-3. An agent or broker can generate underwriting and investment income by forming an agency captive to insure select accounts in response to hard markets. Because the captive is owned by insurance agents or brokers rather than by the insured, the underwriting and investment income from the agency captive flows to the agent or broker.

2-4. Surewell should seek the protection offered by a protected cell company (PCC) as opposed to a rent-a-captive because in a PCC, each participant is assured that the other participants will not be able to access its capital and surplus in the event the cells of those other participants become insolvent. Each participant is also assured that third-party creditors will not access its assets in such a situation. This protection does not necessarily apply to participants in a rent-a-captive structure.

Educational Objective 3

3-1. A captive may help an organization reduce its cost of risk because for the following reasons:
- It involves retention.
- It saves acquisition costs of obtaining insurances.
- It reduces underwriting expenses.
- It specializes in claim adjusting functions.
- It saves the cost of the commercial insurers' overhead and profits.
- It allows for investment income from premium, loss reserve, and collateral investment dollars.

3-2. Having direct access to reinsurers may benefit a captive insurer because reinsurers can be more flexible than insurers in terms of underwriting and rating, the captive can capture the ceding commission on reinsurance, and the insured/owner saves substantial markup costs.

3-3. Adequate risk-shifting and distribution of loss exposures are two key factors the IRS uses to determine whether an insured's premiums paid to the captive insurer are tax-deductible.

3-4. The following are possible disadvantages of using a captive insurance plan:
- Capital requirements and start up costs—Capital of $35,000 to $150,000 must be committed for several years, but the requirement can sometimes be met by using a letter of credit.
- Sensitivity to losses—If the losses retained are higher than forecasted and exceed allocated funds, the financial solvency of the captive could be threatened.
- Pressure from parent company management—The captive must insure the risk required by its parent.
- Payment of premium taxes and residual market loadings—Losses retained are paid for by the parent as a premium on which premium taxes and residual market loadings are levied.

3-5. The firm may gain two advantages if it uses the existence of a captive insurer in its discussions with the commercial insurer. The first is the increased negotiating power it would acquire with its commercial insurer. The commercial insurer may be under the impression that architectural professional liability insurance is hard to place, which may prompt it to charge a higher rate. However, if the commercial insurer learns the insured has the option of using a captive insurer, it may reduce its rate in order to compete with the captive. The second advantage is obtaining rate equity. If historical data predicts that the firm's losses will be substantially lower than the premium being charged, the firm may feel the high rate is a result of the poor loss histories of other firms with which it is pooled. Again, the commercial insurer may be less inclined to assess the firm a higher rate to compensate for the losses from the insurer's other insureds if it knows the firm can obtain from a captive a rate that is more equitable and that more closely resembles a rate based on its predicted losses.

Educational Objective 4

4-1. Actions a risk management professional should perform when conducting a captive insurance plan feasibility study include:
- Obtain an understanding of senior management's objective regarding captive involvement.
- Obtain senior management's approval to enter a captive.
- Analyze the parent company's current risk financing structure.
- Assess the exposure basis of the parent company.
- Assess the parent company's accidental loss history.

4-2. Captive insurers use fronting companies because they provide a way to save the time and expense of obtaining licenses. Captive insurers that use fronting companies operate as reinsurers behind U.S.-licensed insurers.

4-3. The fronting company may require a letter of credit from the captive insurer because the fronting company retains the risk that the captive may not have sufficient funds to reimburse it for payment of covered losses (credit risk). A letter of credit or some other type of financial guarantee offsets the credit risk.

4-4. The premium arrangement between a parent and the captive insurer is as follows:
   a. Guaranteed-cost basis—The insured organization pays a fixed premium rate, transferring the entire loss exposure to its captive.
   b. Retrospectively rated basis—The premium rate adjusts based on a portion of the insured's covered losses during the policy period.

4-5. The following factors should be considered when an organization evaluates the domicile of a captive:
- Minimum premium requirements
- Minimum capitalization
- Solvency requirements
- Incorporation and registration expenses
- Local taxes
- Types of insurance that can be written
- General regulatory environment
- Investment restrictions
- Ease and reliability of communications and travel to and from the domicile
- Political stability
- Support infrastructure in terms of captive managers, claim administrators, bankers, accountants, lawyers, actuaries, and other services

4-6. KYZ's captive insurer assumes the risk that an individual accident/occurrence will fall between $250,000 and $1,000,000. It also assumes the risk that the maximum premium under the incurred loss retrospective rating plan will be exceeded.

Direct Your Learning

Finite and Integrated Risk Insurance Plans

Educational Objectives

After learning the content of this assignment, you should be able to:

1. Describe the characteristics of finite risk insurance plans.
2. Explain how finite risk insurance plans operate, including:
   - Types of risks covered
   - Experience fund terms and calculation guidelines
   - Variations in the terms of plans
3. Describe the advantages and disadvantages of finite risk insurance plans.
4. Describe the financial accounting and tax implications of finite risk insurance plans.
5. Describe the characteristics of integrated risk insurance plans.
6. Explain how integrated risk insurance plans operate, including:
   - Use of the plans
   - Variations in the terms of plans
7. Describe the advantages and disadvantages of integrated risk insurance plans.
8. Describe the characteristics of insured organizations associated with successful finite and integrated risk insurance plans.
9. Define or describe each of the Key Words and Phrases for this assignment.

Study Materials

Required Reading:
- Risk Financing
  - Chapter 9

Study Aids:
- SMART Online Practice Exam
- SMART Study Aids
  - Review Notes and Flash Cards—Assignment 9

Outline

- **Characteristics of Finite Risk Insurance Plans**
- **Operation of Finite Risk Insurance Plans**
    - A. Types of Risk in Finite Risk Insurance Plans
    - B. Experience Fund Terms and Calculation Guidelines
    - C. Use of Finite Risk Insurance Plans
    - D. Variations in the Terms of Finite Risk Plans
        1. Per Occurrence and/or Annual Aggregate Limits
        2. Limits on Annual Loss Payout
        3. Contingent Sharing of Investment Income
        4. Margin Based on a Sliding Scale
        5. Additional Premium Requirement
        6. Prospective Versus Retroactive Plans
        7. Loss Portfolio Transfers
- **Advantages and Disadvantages of Finite Risk Insurance Plans**
- **Financial Accounting and Tax Implications of Finite Risk Insurance Plans**
    - A. Financial Accounting Issues
    - B. Tax Issues
- **Characteristics of Integrated Risk Insurance Plans**
- **Operation of Integrated Risk Insurance Plans**
    - A. Use of Integrated Risk Insurance Plans
    - B. Variations in the Terms of Integrated Risk Insurance Plans
        1. Basket Aggregate Retention
        2. Dual-Trigger Covers
- **Advantages and Disadvantages of Integrated Risk Insurance Plans**
- **Characteristics of Insureds Associated With Successful Finite and Integrated Risk Insurance Plans**
- **Summary**

 Try to establish a study area away from any distractions, to be used only for studying.

For each assignment, you should define or describe each of the Key Words and Phrases and answer each of the Review and Application Questions.

Educational Objective 1
Describe the characteristics of finite risk insurance plans.

Key Words and Phrases
Finite risk insurance plan (p. 9.3)

Commutation (p. 9.4)

Review Questions

1-1. Explain why finite risk insurance plans are frequently referred to as "blended insurance" or "structured programs." (p. 9.3)

1-2. Describe how a finite risk insurance plan differs from a retrospective rating plan. (p. 9.4)

1-3. Why may senior management of an organization that purchases finite risk insurance find the plan's price surprising? (p. 9.4)

Application Question

1-4. Dissatisfied with the standard language offered in traditional insurance policies, Atwell Pharmaceutical's risk management professional tells her broker she wants coverage tailored to the unique needs of her organization. Further, she does not want to renegotiate coverage every year. She also recognizes that a policy written specifically for her organization would be priced based on her organization's frequency/severity profile. What insurance plan may Atwell's risk management professional consider and why?

Educational Objective 2

Explain how finite risk insurance plans operate, including:

- Types of risks covered
- Experience fund terms and calculation guidelines
- Variations in the terms of plans

Key Words and Phrases

Margin (p. 9.5)

Experience fund (p. 9.6)

Underwriting risk (p. 9.8)

Investment risk (p. 9.8)

Timing risk (p. 9.8)

Interest rate risk (p. 9.8)

Credit risk (p. 9.8)

Prospective plan (p. 9.14)

Retroactive plan (p. 9.14)

Loss portfolio transfer (p. 9.14)

Review Questions

2-1. Describe the purpose of an experience fund under a finite risk insurance plan. (p. 9.6)

2-2. Explain how the profit-sharing amount distributed from an experience fund is determined. (p. 9.6)

2-3. Describe the three types of risk present in a finite risk insurance plan. (p. 9.8)

2-4. List the factors an insurer calculates when pricing a guaranteed-cost plan. (p. 9.9)

2-5. Identify the types of situations in which finite risk insurance plans may help control an organization's cost of risk. (p. 9.11)

2-6. Identify factors that affect a finite risk insurance plan's value to an insured. (p. 9.11)

2-7. Describe the following variations in finite risk insurance plan coverage terms: (pp. 9.12–9.14)

   a. Per occurrence and/or annual aggregate limits

   b. Limits on annual loss payout

   c. Contingent sharing of investment income

   d. Margin based on a sliding scale

   e. Additional premium requirement

f. Prospective versus retroactive plans

g. Loss portfolio transfers

Application Question

2-8. Consider the following finite risk insurance plan for XYZ Corporation (XYZ):

Coverage	XYZ's general liability
Limit	$50 million per occurrence/five-year aggregate (including defense costs)
Attachment Point	$10 million per occurrence
Deposit Premium	$6 million /year for five years (total $30 million)
Margin	8 percent of deposit premium (.08 × $30 million), or $2.4 million
Term	Five years, noncancelable
Investment Income Credited	Six-month T-bill rate
Commutation	At the end of five-year policy term and each anniversary thereafter, XYZ has the option to commute the agreement. Upon commutation, any funds returned to XYZ (profit-sharing) are based on the following formula: $30 million deposit premium plus accrued investment income minus the sum of the $2.4 million margin and the paid losses.

a. Explain why XYZ's insurer is taking a limited (finite) amount of risk.

b. Explain how per occurrence and aggregate limits per year could reduce the risk taken by XYZ.

c. Explain how the margin would differ if it were based on a sliding scale.

Educational Objective 3
Describe the advantages and disadvantages of finite risk insurance plans.

Review Questions

3-1. What advantages are associated with implementing a finite risk insurance plan. (p. 9.15)

3-2. Explain how a finite risk insurance plan may help an insured to smooth out losses and premium costs over time. (p. 9.15)

3-3. Explain how a finite risk insurance plan may enable an insured to obtain higher coverage limits. (p. 9.15)

3-4. What disadvantages are associated with implementing a finite risk insurance plan? (p. 9.16)

3-5. Explain how a finite risk insurance plan could cause an organization to incur opportunity cost. (p. 9.16)

Application Question

3-6. Radley Sporting Equipment manufactures football helmets. Its risk management professional is considering a finite risk insurance plan, primarily because of the higher product liability limits it offers compared with traditional insurance plans.
   a. If Radley's risk management professional could reasonably anticipate the company would be subjected to multiple severe losses over the next several years due to an alleged chin strap defect in its helmets, what disadvantage of using a finite risk insurance plan should concern her?

b. What could the risk management professional do to mitigate the disadvantage discussed in (a) above?

Educational Objective 4
Describe the financial accounting and tax implications of finite risk insurance plans.

Key Word or Phrase
EITF 93-6 and *EITF 93-14* (p. 9.19)

Review Questions

4-1. Identify two conditions that must be met in order for an organization to account for a transaction as reinsurance under *FAS 113*. (p. 9.18)

4-2. Contrast the accounting treatment of the annual reinsurance premium if the reinsurance transaction meets or does not meet the standards specified by *FAS 113*. (p. 9.18)

4-3. Explain the significance of *EITF 93-6* and *EITF 93-14* in terms of the accruals the insured and insurer should make at the end of each accounting period if they are treating a finite risk insurance plan as insurance under *FAS 113*. (p. 9.19)

4-4 Identify characteristics of insurance premiums that are tax-deductible, according to the Internal Revenue Service (IRS). (p. 9.20)

Application Question

4-5. Parne Industries, Inc. pays its finite risk insurer a deposit premium of $4 million in the first year of a five-year policy for losses minus a margin of $600,000. Parne's accountants treat the entire deposit premium as insurance. Parne is subsequently audited. The auditors decide only the margin should have been treated as insurance. On what basis may they have made such a determination?

Educational Objective 5

Describe the characteristics of integrated risk insurance plans.

Key Word or Phrase

Integrated risk insurance plan (p. 9.20)

Review Questions

5-1. Identify the types of hazard risk exposures commonly covered by integrated risk insurance plans. (p. 9.20)

5-2. What problems can occur when departmental managers restrict their risk management focus to their individual department's risk exposures? (p. 9.20)

5-3. Explain why a consolidated approach is more financially efficient than an exposure-by-exposure approach to managing risk. (p. 9.21)

Application Question

5-4. Explain how Danforth International, Inc., can benefit from risk diversification and from considering risk on a portfolio basis if in Year 1 it suffers a $250,000 directors and officers liability loss but also realizes a $500,000 gain from a credit risk, while, in Year 2, it has no liability losses but loses $250,000 in commodities value.

Educational Objective 6

Explain how integrated risk insurance plans operate, including:

- Use of the plans
- Variations in the terms of plans

Key Words and Phrases

Basket aggregate retention (p. 9.24)

Dual-trigger cover (p. 9.25)

Review Questions

6-1. Identify the kinds of risks that can be covered using integrated risk insurance plans. (p. 9.23)

6-2. Explain how a basket aggregate retention operates under an integrated risk insurance plan. (p. 9.24)

6-3. Explain the operation of a dual-trigger cover. (p. 9.25)

Application Question

6-4. An integrated risk insurance plan has a limit of $60 million per occurrence and aggregate. It also has a per occurrence retention of $20 million and a limit of $5 million for stop loss cover that attaches above an annual aggregate retention of $30 million. In the following table, enter the values that would apply to this integrated risk insurance plan. (Assume that all the losses are covered under the plan.)

Year	Coverage	Loss	Retained Amount	Stop Loss	Integrated Risk Layer
	Property	$1,000,000	$1,000,000		
1	Marine	2,500,000	2,500,000		
2	Marine	2,000,000	2,000,000		
	Property	80,000,000	20,000,000		60,000,000
	Liability	2,000,000	2,000,000		
	Marine	6,000,000	6,000,000		
3	Marine	3,000,000	2,000,000	1,000,000	
	Liability	32,000,000	20,000,000		12,000,000
4	Crime	1,000,000	1,000,000		
5	Marine	500,000	500,000		
Total		$130,000,000	$57,000,000	$1,000,000	$72,000,000

Educational Objective 7
Describe the advantages and disadvantages of integrated risk insurance plans.

Review Questions

7-1. Identify advantages associated with using an integrated risk insurance plan. (pp. 9.25–9.26)

7-2. Describe how an organization may realize cost savings by using an integrated risk insurance plan. (p. 9.26)

7-3. Identify the disadvantages associated with using an integrated risk insurance plan. (p. 9.26)

Application Question

7-4. Zelles Software creates, sells, delivers and services software programs for its customers. Each of its departments has its own unique needs, which can fluctuate. For example, when programmers in the production department are about to launch a new product, the marketing department has already been busy building demand for it, which exposes the company to possible defamation, breach of warranty, trademark and copyright infringement losses. As the orders for the new product are received, the warehouse and shipping departments also experience a surge in loss exposures (such as workers' compensation and auto liability) when delivering the new product. Several of the company's departments will probably experience an increase in workers' compensation exposure at different levels and at different times. Further, few departments have the same auto liability and delivery exposure as the shipping department or the marketing department's defamation, breach of warranty, trademark, and copyright infringement exposure. How may these circumstances affect whether Zelles uses an integrated risk insurance plan to insure its loss exposures?

Educational Objective 8
Describe the characteristics of insured organizations associated with successful finite and integrated risk insurance plans.

Review Questions

8-1. Explain why finite and integrated risk insurance plans are not suitable for every insured. (p. 9.27)

8-2. Identify characteristics that are likely to contribute to successful development, placement, and implementation of finite and integrated risk insurance plans. (p. 9.27)

8-3. Identify the senior corporate officials instrumental in an insured's successful implementation of finite and integrated risk insurance plans. (p. 9.27)

Answers to Assignment 9 Questions

NOTE: These answers are provided to give students a basic understanding of acceptable types of responses. They often are not the only valid answers and are not intended to provide an exhaustive response to the questions.

Educational Objective 1

1-1. Finite risk insurance plans are frequently referred to as "blended insurance" or "structured programs" due to their combination of retention and transfer components.

1-2. The following is the major difference between a finite risk insurance plan and a retrospective rating plan:
- A finite risk insurance plan usually covers an insured's high-volatility, high-severity losses over several years under a single contract.
- A retrospective rating plan is usually applied to an insured's low-to-medium-severity losses over a single year.

1-3. Senior management may be surprised that the premium percentages of finite risk insurance plans often exceed those of traditional insurance, because the charge is a function of the individual insured's frequency/severity risk profile.

1-4. Atwell's risk management professional may consider a finite risk insurance plan because it meets the following criteria:
- Its manuscript coverage is written to address Atwell's unique needs. The risk protection and policy language are negotiated between the insurer and policyholder.
- Coverage is usually for multiple years, with terms of three to five years the most common.
- Coverage is normally noncancelable except for breaches of contract.
- Premium is generally a substantial percentage of the policy limits because it is based on an organization's individual frequency/severity profile.

Educational Objective 2

2-1. An experience fund under a finite risk insurance plan is used by the insurer to share profit with the insured.

2-2. The profit-sharing amount distributed from an experience fund is determined by adding the premium paid by the insured to the investment income earned and then subtracting the insurer's margin and paid losses.

2-3. The three types of risk involved in a finite risk insurance plan are as follows:
  (1) Underwriting risk—risk that an insurer's losses and expenses will be greater than the premiums and the investment income it expects to earn under the insurance contract
  (2) Investment risk—risk that an insurer's investment income will be lower than it expects and includes timing risk and interest rate risk
  (3) Credit risk—risk that an insurer will not collect premiums owed by its insured

2-4. An insurer calculates the following factors when pricing a guaranteed-cost plan:
- Expected amount of losses
- Expected amount of expenses
- Investment income

2-5. Situations in which finite risk insurance plans may help control an organization's cost of risk include the following:
- Commonly insured property and liability exposures
- Difficult-to-insure exposures
- Uninsurable exposure in an acquisition or a merger situation

2-6. The value of a finite insurance risk plan to an insured depends on the following factors:
- The cost effectiveness and availability of traditional insurance coverage
- Favorable financial accounting
- Beneficial income tax treatment
- Regulatory approval (if needed)
- Management's confidence that the program will provide a material benefit to the company's key stakeholders

2-7. The following variations in terms are used by insurers to tailor an insured's finite risk insurance coverage terms:
   a. Per occurrence and/or annual aggregate limits—Reduce the insurer's risk if per occurrence limits are placed over the term of the agreement or if an aggregate limit is placed over each year.
   b. Limits on annual loss payout—Lower the insurer's investment risk if limits are placed on the annual payout of losses.
   c. Contingent sharing of investment income—Can help align insurer and insured interests and enhances the finite risk transfer partnership when a large interest rate spread between T-Bill rates and other securities is expected.
   d. Margin based on a sliding scale—Instead of a fixed percentage, the insurer receives a fixed margin of the deposit premium based on the loss ratio. This provides the insured with an additional incentive to control losses.
   e. Additional premium requirement—Requires the insured to pay an additional premium if total losses exceed a certain level. Provides economic and cash flow benefits for an insured.
   f. Prospective versus retroactive plans—A prospective plan covers losses from events that have not yet occurred while a retroactive plan covers losses from events that have already occurred.
   g. Loss portfolio transfers—Retroactive plan that applies to an entire portfolio of losses and is used in the reinsurance sector and self-insured organizations.

2-8. a. XYZ's insurer is taking a limited amount of risk because it receives a $30 million premium for writing a policy with an aggregate limit of $50 million. Losses under the policy will probably take several years to settle and be paid, allowing a substantial amount of investment income to accumulate in the experience fund, further limiting the risk taken by XYZ.
   b. A per occurrence limit that is less than the $50 million five-year aggregate limit would reduce the insurer's risk. If there is a $25 million per occurrence limit and a $50 million loss occurs,

the amount paid by the insurer is limited to $25 million. An aggregate limit per year that is less than the $50 million five-year aggregate limit would reduce the risk taken by the insurer.

c. If the margin were based on a sliding scale, it would vary above and below 8 percent based on the relationship between losses and premium (the loss ratio) under the plan. The margin would decrease for favorable loss experience and increase for unfavorable loss experience, giving the insured an incentive to control its losses.

Educational Objective 3

3-1. The following are advantages associated with implementing a finite risk insurance plan:
- Smooths out losses and premium costs over time
- Incorporates features of retention and transfer
- Provides higher coverage limits
- Meets contractual and regulatory requirements
- Reduces the cost and time required for renewals
- Improves risk management budgeting
- Enhances market relationships

3-2. An insured can use a finite risk insurance plan to smooth out losses and premium costs over time by treating the annual premium as an expense on its financial statements and on its income tax returns. It also helps an organization avoid large swings in coverage costs because it fixes premium costs over several years.

3-3. A finite risk insurance plan may enable an insured to obtain higher coverage limits because premiums and limits are combined over several years under a single plan.

3-4. The following are disadvantages associated with implementing a finite risk insurance plan:
- Opportunity cost of capital
- Multiple-year aggregate limit
- Premium taxes
- Difficulty reentering the traditional marketplace
- Regulatory, auditor, and stakeholder scrutiny
- Potentially adverse accounting and tax treatment

3-5. An insured organization should carefully consider the disadvantage of the opportunity cost associated with having its capital tied up in an experience fund associated with a finite risk insurance plan. The cash balance in the experience fund usually is credited with a short-term investment rate based on the three- or six-month T-bill rate. The insured's cost of capital is almost certainly higher than the rate credited to the fund. This results in an opportunity cost to the insured because the insured could have otherwise used the funds as capital and earned a higher rate of return.

3-6. a. Radley's risk management professional should be concerned about the multiple-year aggregate limit. If enough severe losses occur early in the multiyear policy term of the finite risk plan, the aggregate limits could be exhausted before policy term has expired, leaving the company without coverage. Further, the company would be obligated to continue paying the premium.

b. To combat this disadvantage, the risk management professional could negotiate a "limit buy-back" provision that would reinstate the limit of coverage for subsequent losses.

Educational Objective 4

4-1. The following two conditions must be met in order for an organization to account for a transaction as reinsurance under *FAS 113*:

   (1) The reinsurer assumes significant insurance risk under the reinsured portions of the underlying insurance contracts.

   (2) It is *reasonably possible* that the reinsurer may realize a *significant loss* from the transaction.

4-2. For a reinsurance transaction that meets the requirements for reinsurance action under *FAS 113*, the annual reinsurance premium is allowed as an expense on the insurer's financial statements each year.

   For a reinsurance transaction that does not meet the requirements for reinsurance action under *FAS 113*, the insurer must account for the premium as a deposit to fund its losses.

4-3. *EITF 93-6* and *EITF 93-14* suggest making the following accruals at the end of each accounting period if treating a finite risk plan as insurance under *FAS 113*:

   (1) The insured should accrue any experience-related obligations to pay cash or other consideration to the insurer as a liability in its financial statements.

   (2) The insurer should state the insured's experience-related obligations to pay cash or other consideration as an asset in the insurer's financial statements.

   (3) The insured should state any experience-related right to payment from the insurer as an asset in its financial statement.

   (4) The insurer should state the insured's experience-related right to payment as a liability in the insurer's financial statement.

4-4. According to the Internal Revenue Service (IRS), an insurance premium is tax-deductible if it entails both risk-shifting and risk distribution.

4-5. The margin functions like a guaranteed-cost insurance premium, which the insurer used to fund the underwriting and timing risk on a transaction. Based on this reasoning, therefore, the auditors may have believed it was reasonably possible for the insurer under a finite risk plan to realize a significant loss on the margin.

Educational Objective 5

5-1. Integrated risk insurance plans commonly cover financial/market exposures, movements in securities prices, interest rates, and foreign exchange rates.

5-2. This narrow focus ignores the ripple effects of the diverse risks that cross departmental lines or that may have a cumulative effect on the entire organization's hazard, operational and financial risks.

5-3. A consolidated approach is more efficient than an exposure-by-exposure approach in managing risk because the risk taker (the insurer) can diversify its risk across different types of risk exposures and across time, which results in a lower premium.

5-4. Danforth's total net gain or loss over Year 1 and Year 2 for both exposures is $0. Therefore, its combined risk over two years is lower than its net gain or loss on any one risk exposure for any one year.

Educational Objective 6

6-1. Integrated risk insurance plans cover risks that can be accurately modeled, exhibit low or no correlation, and have similar exposure sizes and loss probability profiles.

6-2. Basket aggregate retention is a large aggregate retention spanning multiple types of risk exposure. An integrated risk insurance plan attaches at the point at which the basket aggregate retention is exhausted, and the basket aggregate retention itself sits above separate per occurrence retentions for each type of risk.

6-3. A dual-trigger cover ties an insured's retention and policy limit to two different types of risks, which requires the insured to incur a loss above a certain threshold under each of the two types of risk during the same time period in order to trigger coverage under the policy.

6-4.

Year	Coverage	Loss	Retained Amount	Stop Loss	Integrated Risk Layer
	Property	$1,000,000	$1,000,000		
1	Marine	2,500,000	2,500,000		
2	Marine	2,000,000	2,000,000		
	Property	80,000,000	20,000,000		$60,000,000
	Liability	2,000,000	2,000,000		
	Marine	6,000,000	6,000,000		
3	Marine	3,000,000	2,000,000	$1,000,000	
	Liability	32,000,000	20,000,000		$12,000,000
4	Crime	1,000,000	1,000,000		
5	Marine	500,000	500,000		
Total		$130,000,000	$57,000,000	$1,000,000	$72,000,000

Educational Objective 7

7-1. The following are advantages of using an integrated risk insurance plan:
- Flexibility of coverage
- Cost savings
- Stability
- Greater transparency

7-2. An integrated risk insurance plan offers cost savings through the following:
- Insured's bulk purchasing power
- Absence of annual renewal negotiations
- Reduction of aggregate retained risk through diversification

7-3. The following are disadvantages of using an integrated risk insurance plan:
- Exhaustion of limits with a large loss
- Difficulties in premium allocation
- Complexity of pricing
- Delay in development of specialty policy language
- Reduction of additional services

7-4. Premium allocation among departments of Zelles may be difficult because each department has its own unique risk exposures, making it difficult to allocate a composite premium that transfers risk for several lines together over multiple years under a single contract.

Educational Objective 8

8-1. Finite and integrated risk insurance plans are not suitable for every insured because they require a minimum exposure size, time commitment, significant capital, and possible regulatory approval.

8-2. The following insured characteristics are likely to contribute to successful development, placement, and implementation of finite and integrated risk insurance plans:
- Exposed to difficult- or expensive-to-insure risks that are considered unattractive to the traditional insurance market
- Significant exposure whose associated loss could undermine business stability or have a material effect on net income or other key metrics
- Willing to assume substantial risk retention
- Desire for an innovative, structured solution within the context of an insurance contract
- Senior corporate officials perceive risk transfer to be a priority
- Significant cash on hand and will likely owe taxes

8-3. An insured's senior corporate officials instrumental in the successful implementation of finite and integrated risk insurance plans include key members of the treasury, finance, and legal departments, as well as general management.

Direct Your Learning

Capital Market Risk Financing Plans

Educational Objectives

After learning the content of this assignment, you should be able to:

1. Describe the types of capital market products.
2. Explain how securitization operates.
3. Explain how insurance securitization operates, including:
   - The use of catastrophe bonds
   - The benefits to investors
   - The advantages and disadvantages of insurance securitization
4. Explain how insurance derivatives operate, including:
   - The use of forwards and futures contracts
   - The use of swaps
   - The use of insurance options
   - The advantages and disadvantages of insurance derivatives
5. Explain how contingent capital arrangements operate, including:
   - The use of a standby credit facility
   - The use of a contingent surplus note arrangement
   - The use of a catastrophe equity put arrangement
   - The advantages and disadvantages of contingent capital arrangements
6. Analyze the concerns of organizations transferring risk and investors supplying capital.
7. Explain the regulatory and accounting issues involved with insurance-linked securities and insurance derivatives.
8. Define or describe each of the Key Words and Phrases for this assignment.

Study Materials

Required Reading:
- Risk Financing
  - Chapter 10

Study Aids:
- SMART Online Practice Exam
- SMART Study Aids
  - Review Notes and Flash Cards—Assignment 10

Outline

- **Types of Capital Market Products**
- **Securitization**
- **Insurance Securitizations**
  - A. Catastrophe Bonds
  - B. Benefits to Investors
  - C. Advantages and Disadvantages of Insurance Securitizations
- **Insurance Derivatives**
  - A. Forward Contracts
  - B. Swaps
  - C. Insurance Options
  - D. Advantages and Disadvantages of Insurance Derivatives
- **Contingent Capital Arrangements**
  - A. Standby Credit Facility
  - B. Contingent Surplus Notes
  - C. Catastrophe Equity Put Options
  - D. Advantages and Disadvantages of Contingent Capital Arrangements
- **Concerns of Organizations Transferring Risk and Investors Supplying Capital**
  - A. Organizations Transferring Risk
  - B. Investors Supplying Capital
- **Regulatory and Accounting Issues**
- **Summary**

 Writing notes as you read your materials will help you remember key pieces of information.

For each assignment, you should define or describe each of the Key Words and Phrases and answer each of the Review and Application Questions.

Educational Objective 1
Describe the types of capital market products.

Review Questions

1-1. Identify types of capital market products used to finance risk as an alternative to insurance. (p. 10.3)

1-2. Explain how capital market products provide opportunities to expand the traditional businesses of each of the following organizations: (pp. 10.3–10.4)

   a. Noninsurance financial institutions

   b. Insurers and insurance brokers

1-3. Explain why few large organizations have used capital market products to finance risk. (p. 10.4)

Application Question

1-4. Joyce, the CFO of her organization, believes capital market products can be used to finance any insurable risk. She informs the organization's risk management professional that she wants to use a capital market product to insure the organization's workers' compensation exposure, which constitutes its largest insurance expenditure. Aside from the time and expense required to implement such a coverage plan, what specific concerns may a risk management professional have about adopting such an approach?

Educational Objective 2
Explain how securitization operates.

Key Words and Phrases
Securitization (p. 10.4)

Special purpose vehicle (SPV) (p. 10.4)

Review Questions

2-1. Explain why an organization may benefit from using securitization. (p. 10.4)

2-2. Identify the benefit of using an SPV in a securitization transaction. (p. 10.4)

2-3. Explain why an organization's use of an SPV requires a high level of disclosure regarding the SPV's assets, finances, purpose, and management. (p. 10.5)

Application Question

2-4. Using an example of a bank that issues mortgages, fill in on the dotted lines the appropriate words below to explain the process by which mortgages can be securitized:

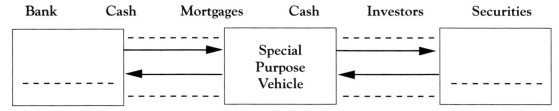

> **Educational Objective 3**
>
> Explain how insurance securitization operates, including:
>
> - The use of catastrophe bonds
> - The benefits to investors
> - The advantages and disadvantages of insurance securitization

Key Words and Phrases

Insurance securitization (p. 10.5)

Catastrophe bonds (p. 10.7)

Basis risk (p. 10.10)

Review Questions

3-1. Describe the role of an insurance-linked security in an insurance securitization. (p. 10.5)

3-2. Explain how an insurance securitization differs from other types of securitization. (p. 10.6)

3-3. Explain why catastrophe bonds are an appealing risk financing technique for bond issuers and bond investors. (p. 10.7)

3-4. Describe how the use of insurance securitizations may affect the following: (pp. 10.9–10.10)

a. An organization's risk transfer capacity

b. An organization's credit risk

3-5. Describe the disadvantages associated with insurance securitization. (pp. 10.9–10.10)

Application Question

3-6. Imagine that you are the chief financial officer of an organization that is considering insurance-linked securities for transferring insurable risk. Place an "X" in each box below that indicates where you would face a trade-off when designing your programs.

	Cost	Moral Hazard
Financial Security (Credit Risk) of the Provider		
Basis Risk		

Educational Objective 4

Explain how insurance derivatives operate, including:

- The use of forwards and futures contracts
- The use of swaps
- The use of insurance options
- The advantages and disadvantages of insurance derivatives

Key Words and Phrases

Insurance derivative (p. 10.11)

Forward contract (p. 10.11)

Swap (p. 10.12)

Option (p. 10.13)

Strike price (p. 10.13)

Call option (p. 10.13)

Put option (p. 10.13)

Insurance option (p. 10.13)

Review Questions

4-1. Explain how the use of a forward contract enables an organization to manage its financial risk effectively. (p. 10.11)

4-2. Describe how an insurer might use a swap to spread its risk. (p. 10.12)

4-3. Describe an option holder's potential gain in the following situations: (p. 10.13)

a. When the value of an underlying asset exceeds the strike price

b. When the value of an underlying asset is below the strike price

4-4. Describe the advantages associated with insurance derivatives. (p. 10.14)

4-5. Describe the disadvantages associated with insurance derivatives. (p. 10.15)

Application Question

4-6. In the following table, answer "yes" or "no" in each box and explain the reasons for your answers.

	Excess Insurance	Insurance Call Option	Insurance Call Option Spread
Purchaser pays premium?			
Allows the purchaser to retain some of its losses?			
Purchaser receives a payment if insurable losses occur and exceed a specified attachment point (or strike value)?			
Has an upper limit?			

Educational Objective 5

Explain how contingent capital arrangements operate, including:

- The use of a standby credit facility
- The use of a contingent surplus note arrangement
- The use of a catastrophe equity put arrangement
- The advantages and disadvantages of contingent capital arrangements

Key Words and Phrases

Contingent capital arrangement (p. 10.16)

Standby credit facility (p. 10.17)

Surplus notes (p. 10.18)

Contingent surplus notes (p. 10.18)

Catastrophe equity put option (p. 10.18)

Review Questions

5-1. Identify factors that influence the amount of capital commitment fee paid in a contingent capital arrangement in exchange for the promise to reimburse loss costs. (p. 10.16)

5-2. Describe the categories of contingent capital agreements.
(p. 10.17)

5-3. Contrast contingent capital arrangements, standby credit facilities, and insurance as risk financing techniques.
(pp. 10.16–10.17)

Application Question

5-4. The executive management of Danford Industries, whose primary headquarters are in an area frequently struck by hurricanes, is trying to determine the best way to insure against the associated catastrophic loss. It favors a contingent capital arrangement because its initial cost of making funds available to the organization in the event of a hurricane is lower than guaranteed-cost insurance's. Danford's management also prefers a contingent capital arrangement because it does not require the organization to maintain a separate reserve for such losses, which reduces opportunity cost. Finally, senior management also likes that the terms of the loan under a contingent capital arrangement, such as its interest rate and payback period, are determined in advance, as opposed to when a catastrophe strikes, which is when creditors may demand much less favorable terms. However, before management adopts a contingent capital arrangement, what disadvantages should the company's risk management professional explain?

10.14 Risk Financing—ARM 56

Educational Objective 6
Analyze the concerns of organizations transferring risk and investors supplying capital.

Key Word or Phrase
Objective trigger (p. 10.22)

Review Questions

6-1. Identify areas of concern for an organization that uses insurance-linked securities and insurance derivatives to transfer risk. (pp. 10.20–10.21)

6-2. Describe the degree of financial security provided by the following products used for risk financing: (p. 10.21)

  a. Traditional and nontraditional

  b. Standardized exchange-traded options

  c. Structured options and swaps

6-3. Describe the relationship between an organization's basis risk and moral hazard in a capital market product transaction. (pp. 10.21–10.22)

Application Question

6-4. The state teachers' pension fund manager would like to supply risk capital through a capital market product for certain industries that she feels are strong enough to endure severe losses. However, she is concerned about moral hazard. Once an organization's losses rise above a certain threshold, at which point the capital market product begins payment, she is concerned it may cease to diligently strive to mitigate its losses. What may an organization that wants to sell the fund manager a capital market product do to convince the fund manager that moral hazard will not be a problem and how will such an action affect the capital market product's price?

Educational Objective 7

Explain the regulatory and accounting issues involved with insurance-linked securities and insurance derivatives.

Review Questions

7-1. Identify the criteria used to determine whether an insurance-linked security or insurance derivative can be considered insurance and regulated as such. (pp. 10.22–10.23)

7-2. Describe the difference in regulatory and accounting treatment for insurance-linked securities and insurance derivatives that are determined to be insurance and those that are determined not to be insurance. (p. 10.23)

7-3. Explain how the use of a special purpose vehicle (SPV) provides the organization transferring its risk with tax and accounting advantages. (p. 10.23)

Application Question

7-4. Write "yes" or "no" in each box below to explain how the regulatory and accounting treatments of insurance-linked securities and insurance derivatives differ depending on whether they are considered to be insurance.

	Insurance	Not Insurance
Must comply with state insurance regulations?		
State premium taxes must be paid?		
Amount paid to transfer risk is tax-deductible?		
Required to record on the balance sheet outstanding loss liabilities covered by the insurance-linked securities and insurance derivatives?		

Answers to Assignment 10 Questions

NOTE: These answers are provided to give students a basic understanding of acceptable types of responses. They often are not the only valid answers and are not intended to provide an exhaustive response to the questions.

Educational Objective 1

1-1. The following types of capital market products are commonly used as alternatives to insurance to finance risk:
- Insurance-linked securities
- Insurance derivatives
- Contingent capital arrangements

1-2. Capital market products provide opportunities to expand traditional business in the following ways:
   a. Noninsurance financial institutions expand their traditional business by offering the capital markets' capacity to organizations as an alternative to using insurance to finance losses.
   b. Insurers (and reinsurers) and insurance brokers expand their traditional business by using insurance policies and/or capital market products to cover not only losses from traditionally insurable risks, but also losses from other types of risk, such as commodity price risk and interest rate risk.

1-3. Few large organizations have used capital market products to finance risk because they involve a great deal of time and expense to implement.

1-4. Writing workers' compensation insurance through a capital market product may not be feasible unless sufficient underwriting data exist. A bigger hurdle for the workers' compensation coverage may be obtaining regulatory approval and determining the appropriate accounting treatment for such a plan.

Educational Objective 2

2-1. An organization may use securitization to exchange income-producing assets for cash provided by the purchaser of the security, allowing the organization to transfer the asset from its balance sheet in exchange for cash, which is more versatile.

2-2. The benefit of using a special purpose vehicle in a securitization transaction is that investors can decide whether to invest in the securities based solely on the risk presented by the income-producing assets held as collateral by the SPV.

2-3. An organization's use of an SPV requires a high level of disclosure because SPVs can be used to manipulate the organization's income statement or balance sheet. To assure regulators, auditors, and potential investors, the organization must meet all regulatory requirements and maintain a high level of disclosure regarding the SPV's assets, finances, purpose, and management.

2-4.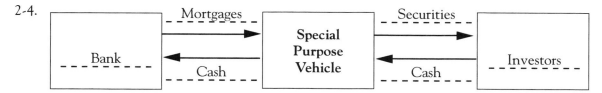

Educational Objective 3

3-1. An insurance-linked security in an insurance securitization creates a marketable insurance-linked security based on the cash flows that arise from insuring loss exposures. The cash flows are similar to premium and loss payments under an insurance policy.

3-2. An insurance securitization differs from other types of securitization because the organization pays cash to the SPV and receives reimbursement for losses that occur. When reimbursement is based on actual losses, the insurance securitization transaction mimics a traditional insurance risk transfer.

3-3. Catastrophe bonds appeal to both the bond issuers and bond investors because the bond issuers want them triggered and priced at a level that reflects a highly infrequent event. Investors want them to respond to highly infrequent events because that lowers the risk that they will lose money on their investment.

3-4. The use of insurance securitizations may have the following effects:

   a. Insurance securitizations may create additional risk transfer capacity by supplementing an organization's existing risk-transfer capacity and providing an alternative to traditional insurance and reinsurance.

   b. Insurance securitizations may lower credit risk because the obligation to pay losses to an organization and to pay interest and principal to investors is fully collateralized with investments held by the SPV, which can be readily converted into cash.

3-5. Disadvantages associated with insurance securitization include the following:
   - They expose an organization to the volatility of the market's demand.
   - They entail opportunity costs of collateralized assets.
   - They involve substantial transaction costs.
   - They subject organizations to basis risk.

3-6.

	Cost	Moral Hazard
Financial Security (Credit Risk) of the Provider	X	
Basis Risk	X	X

Educational Objective 4

4-1. The use of a forward contract helps an organization effectively manage its financial risk because it enables a buyer and seller of a commodity to know its price prior to delivery. The risk of price fluctuations of the commodity subject to the futures contract is reduced and the organization is able to plan and budget activities with less concern regarding price changes.

4-2. An insurer might use a swap arrangement to spread or diversify its risk. The swap becomes an insurance derivative with the underlying asset a portfolio of a specified class of insured risks for an individual insurer. The insurer may able to limit exposure to specific geographic catastrophes and enhance the diversification of their portfolios.

4-3. The relationship between the value of a call option and the value of an underlying asset is as follows:

a. When the value of an option's underlying asset exceeds the strike price, the buyer can exercise (sell) and realize a gain.

b. When the value of an option's underlying asset is less than the strike price, the buyer cannot realize a gain by exercising the option.

4-4. Advantages associated with insurance derivatives include the following:
- Additional risk capacity
- Lower in cost than insurance-linked securities
- Transparent pricing
- Opportunities for investors to exit during its term
- Standardized contracts
- Efficient claims and contract settlement

4-5. Disadvantages associated with insurance derivatives include the following:
- Underdeveloped markets
- Basis risk
- Credit risk
- Uncertain regulatory and accounting treatment

4-6.

	Excess Insurance	Insurance Call Option	Insurance Call Option Spread
Purchaser pays premium?	Yes	Yes	Yes
Allows the purchaser to retain some of its losses?	Yes	Yes	Yes
Purchaser receives a payment if insurable losses occur and exceed a specified attachment point (or strike value)?	Yes	Yes	Yes
Has an upper limit?	Yes	No	Yes

Excess insurance, insurance call options, and insurance call option spreads have similar characteristics except, theoretically, an insurance call option has no limit.

Educational Objective 5

5-1. Factors that influence the amount of capital commitment fee paid in a contingent capital arrangement include:
- Likeliness of a loss event
- Interest rates of alternative investments
- Credit risk of the organization trying to arrange for the contingent capital

5-2. Contingent capital agreements fall into one of the following categories:
- Standby credit facility—Provides prearranged credit to an organization in the event the organization suffers a loss. Interest rate and principal repayment schedules are known in advance of a loss.
- Contingent surplus note—Increases an insurer's assets without increasing its liabilities, which may result in an increase in capacity to sell business.
- Catastrophe equity put option—Provides a way for an insurer or a noninsurance organization to raise funds in the event of a catastrophic loss by providing a right to sell equity (stock) at a predetermined price in the event of a catastrophe loss.

5-3. Used as a risk financing technique, standby credit facility entails loss retention because it obligates the organization to pay back, with interest, a loan it uses to cover losses. Insurance entails loss transfer because the funds it supplies do not have to be repaid.

5-4. Danford's risk management professional should explain that accurate loss forecasting is critical because if its expected losses exceed its guaranteed-cost insurance premium, insurance is the best option. This is the case because insurance is not loss sensitive and the funds it supplies would not have to be repaid, unlike the loan created by the contingent capital arrangement. Further, if equity were issued instead of debt, as would be the case with guaranteed-cost insurance, ownership of Danford would not be diluted. The ownership dilution that results from a contingent capital arrangement could occur as Danford tries to recover from a catastrophe.

Educational Objective 6

6-1. Areas of concern for an organization using insurance-linked securities and insurance derivatives to transfer risk include cost, financial security (credit risk) of the parties supplying the risk capital, and the risk that the amount received may not match the amount of its loss (basis risk).

6-2. The degrees of financial security provided by products used for risk financing include:
   a. Traditional and nontraditional insurance—high level of financial security because they are fully collateralized
   b. Standardized exchange-traded options—high level of financial security guaranteed by the exchange on which they are traded
   c. Structured options and swaps—low level of financial security, depending on the financial strength of the other party (the counterparty) to the transaction

6-3. In capital market product transactions, generally the lower the degree of an organization's basis risk, the higher the degree of moral hazard.

6-4. The organization can offer to use an objective trigger, which is a measurement that determines the value of an insurance-related capital market product based on a parameter that is not within the control of the organization transferring the risk. The increased basis risk should reduce the cost to the organization transferring the risk.

Educational Objective 7

7-1. The following criteria are used to determine whether an insurance-linked security or insurance derivative can be considered insurance and regulated as insurance:

- The contract must indemnify an organization for its actual losses.
- The insured organization must have an insurable interest that is the subject of an insurance contract.

Insurance securitizations and insurance derivatives whose values are based on an objective trigger may not be considered insurance and should not be regulated as insurance.

7-2. Regulatory and accounting treatment for insurance-linked securities and insurance derivatives that are determined to be insurance must comply with insurance regulations. The organization could deduct state premium taxes and it would not be required to record outstanding losses that are covered by the insurance on the liability section of the balance sheet.

Investors in insurance-linked securities and insurance derivatives that are not determined to be insurance must comply with the requirements of the various regulators of securities and derivatives. The organization would not be able to deduct for tax purposes the amount it pays to transfer risk and the organization must record on its balance sheet outstanding losses that are meant to be covered by the proceeds from the insurance-linked security or insurance derivative. The organization can show a corresponding asset on its balance sheet for the fair value of the insurance-linked security or insurance derivative

7-3. An organization transferring its risk of loss through a SPV may have the transaction treated as insurance or reinsurance if the SPV qualifies as an insurer or a reinsurer under U.S. state regulations.

7-4.

	Insurance	Not Insurance
Must comply with state insurance regulations?	Yes	No
State premium taxes must be paid?	Yes	No
Amount paid to transfer risk is tax-deductible?	Yes	No
Required to record on the balance sheet outstanding loss liabilities covered by the insurance-linked securities and insurance derivatives?	No	Yes

Direct Your Learning

Noninsurance Contractual Transfer of Risk

Educational Objectives

After learning the content of this assignment, you should be able to:

1. Describe the types of noninsurance risk transfers and several examples of each type.

2. Describe noninsurance risk control and risk financing transfers categorized by type of transaction.

3. Describe noninsurance risk financing transfers categorized by how they alter common-law liabilities.

4. Describe the legal principles underlying noninsurance risk control and risk financing transfers.

5. Explain how to manage noninsurance risk control and risk financing transfers.

6. Define or describe each of the Key Words and Phrases for this assignment.

Study Materials

Required Reading:
- Risk Financing
  - Chapter 11

Study Aids:
- SMART Online Practice Exam
- SMART Study Aids
  - Review Notes and Flash Cards—Assignment 11

Outline

- **Types of Noninsurance Risk Transfers**
  - A. Noninsurance Risk Control Transfers
    1. Incorporation
    2. Leasing
    3. Contracting for Services
    4. Suretyship and Guaranty Agreements
    5. Waivers
    6. Limitations of Liability
    7. Disclaimer of Warranties
  - B. Noninsurance Risk Financing Transfers
    1. Hold-Harmless Agreements
    2. Transfer of Risk to the Transferee's Insurer
- **Noninsurance Risk Control and Risk Financing Transfers—Type of Transaction**
  - A. Construction Contracts
  - B. Service and Maintenance Contracts
  - C. Purchase Order Contracts
  - D. Lease of Premises Contracts
  - E. Equipment Lease Contracts
  - F. Bailment Contracts
  - G. Sale and Supply Contracts
- **Noninsurance Risk Financing Transfers—How They Alter Common-Law Liabilities**
  - A. Transferring Responsibility for Joint Fault (Limited Form)
  - B. Transferring All Responsibility Except Transferor's Fault (Intermediate Form)
  - C. Transferring All Responsibility (Broad Form)
- **Legal Principles Underlying Noninsurance Risk Transfers**
  - A. Freedom of Contract
  - B. Common-Law Limitations
    1. Unconscionability
    2. Public Policy
  - C. Statutory Limitations
    1. All-Inclusive Statutes
    2. Statutes Prohibiting Particular Wording
    3. Statutes Prescribing Certain Wording
- **Management of Noninsurance Risk Control and Risk Financing Transfers**
  - A. Factors Affecting Appropriate Use of Noninsurance Risk Transfers
    1. Enforceability
    2. Ability to Manage Risk
    3. Consideration Paid
  - B. Elements of a Noninsurance Risk Transfer Program
    1. General Administrative Controls
    2. Records of Contractual Transfers
    3. Specific Control Measures
  - C. Fundamental Guidelines
- **Summary**

 Before starting a new assignment, briefly review the Educational Objectives of those preceding it.

For each assignment, you should define or describe each of the Key Words and Phrases and answer each of the Review and Application Questions.

Educational Objective 1
Describe the types of noninsurance risk transfers and several examples of each type.

Key Words and Phrases

Noninsurance risk control transfer (p. 11.4)

Noninsurance risk financing transfer (p. 11.5)

Segregation (p. 11.6)

Leasehold (p. 11.7)

Sale-and-lease-back arrangement (p. 11.8)

Surety (p. 11.9)

Obligee (p. 11.9)

Principal, or obligor (p. 11.9)

Guarantor (p. 11.10)

Exoneration (p. 11.11)

Subrogation (in a surety agreement) (p. 11.11)

Indemnity (in a surety agreement) (p. 11.11)

Waiver (p. 11.12)

Exculpatory clause (p. 11.12)

Waiver of subrogation (p. 11.13)

Indemnitor (p. 11.15)

Indemnitee (p. 11.15)

Additional insured endorsement (p. 11.16)

Named insured endorsement (p. 11.16)

Review Questions

1-1. Describe two categories of noninsurance risk transfers. (pp. 11.4–11.5)

1-2. Identify three situations in which the party who hires an independent contractor is liable for the torts of that contractor for an injury to a third party. (pp. 11.8–11.9)

1-3. Contrast the protection granted to the obligee in the following agreements: (pp. 11.9–11.10)
   a. Surety agreement

   b. Guaranty agreement

1-4. Identify two ways in which a surety agreement differs from most insurance contracts. (p. 11.10)

1-5. Describe how the following rights protect a surety against loss from the principal's misconduct or from collusion between the principal and the obligee: (p. 11.11)
   a. Exoneration

   b. Subrogation

   c. Indemnity

1-6. List the criteria that a waiver must meet in order to be effective. (p. 11.12)

1-7. Identify the purposes served by including a disclaimer of warranties in a sales contract. (pp. 11.13–11.14)

1-8. Describe the following two endorsements that modify an insurance agreement to transfer risk to a transferee's insurer: (pp. 11.16–11.17)

　　a. Additional insured endorsement

　　b. Named insured endorsement

Application Question

1-9. Chopper Corporation, a manufacturer of helicopters, purchases altimeters for its aircraft from Instrument Corporation. Because the safety of a helicopter depends on the accuracy of its altimeter, Chopper Corporation is considering requiring Instrument Corporation to sign an agreement to indemnify it for any claims, related legal expenses, and other costs it may incur because of an altimeter malfunction. From Chopper Corporation's standpoint, would such an agreement be an application of risk control or risk financing?

Educational Objective 2
Describe noninsurance risk control and risk financing transfers categorized by type of transaction.

Key Words and Phrases

Bailment (p. 11.21)

Bailee (p. 11.21)

Bailor (p. 11.21)

Mutual benefit bailment (p. 11.21)

Gratuitous bailment (p. 11.21)

Free on Board (F.O.B.) (p. 11.23)

Cost-insurance Freight (C.I.F.) (p. 11.24)

Installment or conditional sales contract (p. 11.24)

Fungible goods (p. 11.24)

Review Questions

2-1. Explain why a risk management professional should be aware of transfers of risk control or risk financing in an organization's contractual agreements. (pp. 11.17–11.18)

2-2. Identify the types of contracts that may contain noninsurance risk transfers. (p. 11.18)

2-3. Describe how the level of liability on a mutual benefit bailment may be contractually altered by the following parties: (p. 11.21)

a. Bailee

b. Bailor

2-4. Describe how the following contracts transfer risk between the buyers and the sellers of goods: (pp. 11.22–11.24)

a. Consignment

b. Conditional sales contract

Application Question

2-5. A manufacturer in Chicago regularly ships goods to a customer in Atlanta. Explain how each of the following terms of shipment in the sales agreement prepared by the manufacturer affects the allocation of exposures to damage to the goods while in transit.

a. F.O.B. Chicago

b. F.O.B. Atlanta

c. C.I.F.

Educational Objective 3

Describe noninsurance risk financing transfers categorized by how they alter common-law liabilities.

Review Questions

3-1. Identify the three forms of contract provisions that alter common-law liabilities affecting a transferor's potential or actual liability loss exposures. (p. 11.25)

3-2. Describe the extent of responsibility transferred by the limited, the intermediate, and the broad noninsurance risk financing transfers. (pp. 11.25–11.27)

3-3. Identify to whom financial liability for a claim is transferred with each type of noninsurance risk financing transfer form. (pp. 11.25–11.27)

Application Question

3-4. Green Acres retirement home hires the Smith Contracting Company to enlarge the facility's dining room. The management of Green Acres wants to add a noninsurance risk financing transfer agreement to protect it against all claims except those that are its fault. What type of noninsurance risk financing transfer form would be appropriate for transferring this level of common-law liability?

Educational Objective 4

Describe the legal principles underlying noninsurance risk control and risk financing transfers.

Key Words and Phrases

Unconscionable provision (p. 11.28)

Public policy (p. 11.28)

Review Questions

4-1. Explain the importance of the freedom of contract and imposing certain limitations in noninsurance risk transfers. (p. 11.27)

4-2. Identify noninsurance risk transfers that courts commonly refuse to enforce. (pp. 11.27–11.28)

4-3. Identify three actions states apply to noninsurance risk transfer contracts to promote fairness and appropriate allocations of loss exposures and actual losses. (p. 11.27)

Application Question

4-4. When he was hired at Meat Packing Inc., Jack Cross was required to sign a contract stating that if he were injured at work, he would waive his workers' compensation benefits. Would Meat Packing Inc.'s inclusion of such a clause in the employment contract satisfy the legal principles underlying noninsurance risk transfers?

Educational Objective 5

Explain how to manage noninsurance risk control and risk financing transfers.

Review Questions

5-1. List the measures a risk management professional may implement to achieve consistent and effective control of an organization's noninsurance risk transfers. (p. 11.33)

5-2. Identify the three factors a risk management professional should consider when seeking fair and mutually beneficial noninsurance risk transfers. (p. 11.33)

5-3. Identify questions a risk management professional should consider, for the purpose of administrative control, when reviewing and evaluating noninsurance risk transfer contracts. (p. 11.37)

5-4. List guidelines an organization should follow when managing noninsurance risk transfers. (p. 11.38)

Application Question

5-5. XYZ Corporation sells medical equipment. It enters into new contracts daily. What should a newly hired risk management professional do to identify and evaluate the noninsurance risk transfer agreements that may exist in the organization's contracts?

Answers to Assignment 11 Questions

NOTE: These answers are provided to give students a basic understanding of acceptable types of responses. They often are not the only valid answers and are not intended to provide an exhaustive response to the questions.

Educational Objective 1

1-1. The following are two broad types of noninsurance risk transfers:
- Noninsurance risk control transfer—transfers a loss exposure from transferor to transferee, thereby eliminating the possibility that the transferor will suffer a loss from the transferred exposure
- Noninsurance risk financing transfer—transfers the financial burden of losses from the transferor to the transferee by obligating the transferee to pay money to (or on behalf of) the transferor after the transferor or some third party has suffered a loss

1-2. In the following three situations, the party who hires an independent contractor is liable for the torts of that contractor for an injury to a third party:
   (1) If the party that hired the contractor is negligent in selecting the contractor, giving directions, or failing to stop any unnecessary dangerous practices that come to the contractor's attention
   (2) If the responsibility that certain duties, commonly created by statute, contract, or common law, be performed safely cannot be delegated to another party
   (3) If the subcontracted work is inherently dangerous to others

1-3. The rights an obligee are protected by the following agreements:
   a. Surety agreement—protects the obligee by providing a second source of performance as soon as the principal's failure to perform becomes apparent
   b. Guaranty agreement—provides a promise to perform a duty in the event the party whose duty it was initially fails to perform only after the obligee has made every reasonable and legal effort to compel the principal's performance

1-4. The following are two ways a surety agreement differs from most insurance contracts:
   (1) The surety's primary obligation is to perform as promised for the obligee, not to pay money to compensate the obligee for the principal's breach of contract.
   (2) A surety agreement is a three-party contract; virtually all insurance policies are two-party contracts.

1-5. The following rights protect a surety against loss from the principal's misconduct or from collusion between the principal and the obligee:
   a. Exoneration—surety released from its liability to the extent that the surety can show that the obligee's inaction increased the surety's loss or otherwise harmed the surety
   b. Subrogation—entitles the surety to the same payment the defaulting principal would have received
   c. Indemnity—entitles a surety to seek reimbursement from the principal for the resources the surety expended when it performed the principal's duty

1-6. For a waiver to be effective, the following criteria must be met:
- The waiving party must not have been forced to sign it by uneven bargaining power.
- It must be obtained honestly, not by deceit or concealment.
- It must state the specific right that is being waived in a clear and unambiguous manner.
- It must be supported by legal consideration paid to the party waiving the right.

1-7. Including a disclaimer of warranties in a sales contract may serve the following purposes:
- To deny any express warranties made in conjunction with the property's sale
- To deny several warranties that by default are often implied, such as for purpose or merchantability

1-8. The following two endorsements modify an insurance agreement to transfer risk to a transferee's insurer:
   a. Additional insured endorsement—adds coverage for one or more persons or organizations to the named insured's policy
   b. Named insured endorsement—adds coverage for one or more persons or organizations to the named insured's policy and elevates the new insured to the status of a named insured, giving it special rights and obligations

1-9. An agreement to indemnify Chopper Corporation for any claims and related legal expenses and other costs it may incur because of an altimeter malfunction would be considered a risk financing transfer. The loss exposure is not transferred by such an agreement but the financial consequences of a loss caused by a malfunctioning altimeter are transferred from Chopper Corporation to Instrument Corporation.

Educational Objective 2

2-1. A risk management professional should be aware of contractual transfers of risk control or risk financing contained in an organization's contractual agreements because they could contain conflicts that could render the transfers meaningless.

2-2. The following types of contracts may contain noninsurance risk transfers:
- Construction contracts
- Service and maintenance contracts
- Purchase order contracts
- Lease of premises contracts
- Equipment lease contracts
- Bailment contracts
- Sale and supply contracts

2-3. The level of liability on a mutual benefit bailment may be limited in the following ways:
   a. Bailee—seeks to limit liability through posted notices or contract provisions stating it is not responsible for damage to a bailor's goods
   b. Bailor—seeks to increase the bailee's liability by holding the bailee responsible for specified acts of God

2-4. Transfer of risk between buyers and sellers of goods is as follows for the corresponding contracts:
   a. Consignment—Title to the property is placed with the manufacturer or processor until the distributor sells the goods to the retailer or ultimate consumer. The distributor is never exposed to loss from their damage or destruction.
   b. Conditional sales contract—The seller usually retains title. Exposure to loss because of property damage can be transferred immediately to the buyer by the sales contract.

2-5. The following terms of shipment in the sales agreement prepared by the manufacturer affect the allocation of exposures to damage to the goods while in transit to Atlanta:
   a. F.O.B. Chicago—absolves the manufacturer in Chicago of responsibility for goods sold once they have reached Atlanta
   b. F.O.B. Atlanta—customer in Atlanta owns and is responsible for the loss of goods when they reach Atlanta and are ready to be unloaded
   c. C.I.F.—customer in Atlanta acquires ownership as soon as the goods are on board the ship; manufacturer must purchase sufficient insurance and pay for the freight

Educational Objective 3

3-1. The following are three forms of contract provisions that alter common-law liabilities affecting a transferor's potential or actual liability loss exposures:
   (1) Transferring responsibility for joint fault (limited form)
   (2) Transferring all responsibility except transferor's fault (intermediate form)
   (3) Transferring all responsibility (broad form)

3-2. The extent of responsibility transferred by noninsurance risk transfers is as follows:
   - Limited form—One contracting party transfers its common-law responsibility for joint civil wrongs to the other contracting party. The transferee must agree to hold the transferor harmless from claims arising from their joint fault.
   - Intermediate form—Protects the transferor from all claims except those arising from the transferor's sole fault.
   - Broad form—Places responsibility for all financial consequences of potential losses on the transferee.

3-3. The limited and intermediate forms seek to progressively improve the transferor's position, transferring ever greater financial consequences to the transferee. The broad form attempts to transfer all financial consequences of potential losses to the transferee.

3-4. An intermediate form would protect against all claims except those arising from the fault of Green Acres.

Educational Objective 4

4-1. Allowing certain freedoms in noninsurance risk transfers is important because they promote commerce and facilitate business transactions. Limitations imposed by common law and statutes are important because they protect the public by preventing contracting parties from engaging in unacceptable behavior.

4-2. Courts commonly refuse to enforce the following types of noninsurance risk transfers:
- Transfers that have been unfairly imposed
- Transfers that unreasonably interfere with the rights of others who are not parties to the contract

4-3. Three actions applied by states to noninsurance risk transfer contracts to promote fairness and appropriate allocations of loss exposures include the following:
(1) Prohibiting certain types of transfers in some contracts
(2) Prohibiting certain wording in some forms of contractual transfers
(3) Prescribing the wording of transfer provisions

4-4. No, such a waiver would not satisfy the legal principles underlying noninsurance risk transfers because such a clause would require the employee to waive rights without providing an alternative method of compensation, which would be contrary to the goal of workers' compensation statutes. The financial responsibility of income loss would fall to society rather than on the employer.

Educational Objective 5

5-1. Measures a risk management professional may implement to achieve consistent and effective control of an organization's noninsurance risk transfers include the following:
- An analysis of factors affecting appropriate use of risk transfers
- A clearly written and widely disseminated organizational policy with general administrative controls and specific control measures for managing noninsurance transfers

5-2. A risk management professional should consider the following three factors in seeking fair and mutually beneficial noninsurance risk transfers:
(1) The legal enforceability of contract provisions
(2) The relative abilities of the parties to mange risk
(3) The price or other legal consideration the transferor explicitly or implicitly pays or gives to the transferee

5-3. A risk management professional should consider the following questions when reviewing and evaluating risk transfer contracts:
- To what extent can the assumption of loss exposure be reduced?
- What loss exposure can the organization safely assume?
- To what extent should contractually assumed loss exposures be transferred by insurance?
- Can specific contract provisions be deleted, particularly those involving loss exposures that can be neither safely retained nor transferred?
- Can clearer contract language be negotiated, especially to clarify points that seem likely to be disputed?

5-4. An organization should use the following guidelines when managing noninsurance risk transfers:
- Ensure that the indemnitor can fulfill its commitment financially
- Require a certificate of insurance for contractual liability coverage before contract operation begins
- Be named as an additional insured on the transferee's policy

- Avoid being too severe
- Avoid ambiguity
- Become more actively involved in legislation

5-5. First, XYZ's risk management professional should apply general administrative controls to the more common routine contracts, such as purchase orders and service agreements. These contracts should be reviewed by experienced personnel. Wording should be standardized. Subsequent periodic audits will likely be sufficient. Nonroutine contracts require more attention. Education and training for all responsible personnel is important because risk transfers in agreements are not always easy to spot or evaluate. Such transfers could adversely affect XYZ. These types of contracts require more than periodic auditing.

Second, records of contractual risk transfers are needed, which include copies of the contracts, identification of the parties to whom XYZ is bound and from whom XYZ is to entitled to protection. These records are likely voluminous and frequently subject to change. Therefore, a computerized risk management information system (RMIS) can be helpful.

Direct Your Learning

Purchasing Insurance and Other Risk Financing Services

Educational Objectives

After learning the content of this assignment, you should be able to:

1. Describe the six steps in purchasing insurance and other risk financing services.
2. Explain the marketing considerations for risk financing plans.
3. Describe the types, roles, required characteristics, and compensation of risk financing plan intermediaries.
4. Describe the opportunities for unbundling the services that are part of an insurance package.
5. Explain how to evaluate proposal responses, including:
   - Services offered
   - Financial stability of insurers
   - Costs
6. Describe the legal principles of insurance contracts.
7. Define or describe each of the Key Words and Phrases for this assignment.

Study Materials

Required Reading:
- Risk Financing
  - Chapter 12

Study Aids:
- SMART Online Practice Exam
- SMART Study Aids
  - Review Notes and Flash Cards—Assignment 12

Outline

- **Steps in Purchasing Insurance and Other Risk Financing Services**
    A. Determination of Insurance Needs and Development of Specifications for Coverage
    B. Presentation to Insurers Through Intermediaries
    C. Development and Presentation of Coverage Proposals by Insurers and Intermediaries
    D. Evaluation of Coverage Proposals by the Organization
    E. Entrance Into an Insurance Contract Between the Organization and the Insurer
    F. Implementation of the New Insurance Coverage
- **Risk Financing Plan Marketing Considerations**
    A. Nature of Insurance Marketing
    B. Market Timing Considerations
        1. Frequency
        2. Scheduling
    C. Insurance Specifications
        1. Format
        2. Content
    D. Competitive Bidding
- **Risk Financing Plan Intermediaries**
    A. Types of Intermediaries
        1. Broker
        2. Agent
        3. Direct Writing Insurer
        4. Risk Management Consultant
    B. Required Characteristics of Intermediaries
        1. Technical Expertise
        2. Financial Resources
        3. Creativity
        4. Agreement on Claim Settlement Approach
        5. Integrity
    C. Compensation of Intermediaries
- **Opportunities for Unbundling Services**
    A. Claim Administration Services
    B. Risk Control Services
    C. Risk Management Information Services (RMIS)
    D. Financial Management Services
    E. Multiple Intermediary Marketing Services
    F. Actuarial Services
- **Evaluation of Coverage Proposals**
    A. Services Offered
    B. Financial Stability
    C. Costs
- **Legal Principles of Insurance Contracts**
    A. Disclosure
        1. Misrepresentation
        2. Concealment
        3. Breach of Warranty
        4. Statutory Modifications
    B. Equity
        1. Waiver and Estoppel
        2. Contract of Adhesion
        3. Unconscionable Advantage and Reasonable Expectations
        4. Correction of Mistakes
        5. Conditional Contracts
    C. Indemnity
        1. Pay for Actual Loss
        2. Require an Insurable Interest
        3. Prevent Duplicate Coverage
        4. Allow Subrogation
- **Summary**

Perform a final review before your exam, but don't cram. Give yourself between two and four hours to go over the course work.

Purchasing Insurance and Other Risk Financing Services   12.3

For each assignment, you should define or describe each of the Key Words and Phrases and answer each of the Review and Application Questions.

Educational Objective 1

Describe the six steps in purchasing insurance and other risk financing services.

Key Word or Phrase

Intermediary (p. 12.3)

Review Questions

1-1. Identify the six steps commonly involved in purchasing risk financing services. (pp. 12.3–12.4)

1-2. Describe how a risk management professional determines specifications for exposures that will not be retained or transferred to a noninsurance transferee. (pp. 12.4–12.5)

1-3. Identify factors that determine who in an organization has authority to accept an insurer's coverage proposal. (p. 12.7)

Application Question

1-4. Tarnely is the risk management professional for Millwright Industries. He has performed the first step in the insurance purchase process, having determined the insurance needs of Millwright and developed the specifications for coverage. He is now ready to present Millwright's proposal for coverage to insurers through intermediaries. He knows he must do this carefully because certain coverages may be hard to place due to a hard market and Millwright's poor workers' compensation loss history. What tasks should Tarnely perform to be sure Millwright's proposal is presented appropriately?

Educational Objective 2

Explain the marketing considerations for risk financing plans.

Key Words and Phrases

Open bidding (p. 12.14)

Closed, or selective bidding (p. 12.14)

Review Questions

2-1. Identify the marketing issues a risk management professional should consider when placing or renewing insurance. (p. 12.7)

2-2. Identify the marketing activities that a risk management professional should perform. (p. 12.8)

2-3. Describe how an organization may obtain insurance using the following two categories of bidding: (pp. 12.14–12.15)
   a. Open bidding

   b. Closed, or selective, bidding

Application Question

2-4. Danford Insurance has provided insurance coverage for Gallon Manufacturing in the small town of Tiny, Pa., for the last ten years. Management has been satisfied with the coverage and premium rates provided by Danford. Explain why Gallon may prefer selective bidding of insurance accounts rather than open bidding at the renewal of its policies.

Educational Objective 3

Describe the types, roles, required characteristics, and compensation of risk financing plan intermediaries.

Key Words and Phrases

Broker (p. 12.15)

Agent (p. 12.16)

Direct writing insurer (p. 12.16)

Risk management consultant (p. 12.16)

Sliding scale commission (p. 12.21)

Management fee (p. 12.21)

Review Questions

3-1. Identify the four primary types of intermediaries an organization may use to obtain insurance coverage. (p. 12.15)

3-2. List activities a risk management consultant is commonly hired to perform. (pp. 12.16–12.17)

3-3. Identify required characteristics for the broker, agent, direct writing insurer, or risk management consultant. (pp. 12.17–12.18)

3-4. Describe the following methods of compensation used for intermediaries: (pp. 12.21–12.22)

a. Sliding scale commission

b. Management fee

Application Question

3-5. A broker wants to convince the risk management professional for Parne, Inc., that she should hire him because he is willing to be compensated on a fee-for-service basis. The argument for commission-based compensation aside, how may Parne benefit from such an arrangement?

Educational Objective 4
Describe the opportunities for unbundling the services that are part of an insurance package.

Key Word or Phrase
Unbundling (p. 12.22)

Review Questions

4-1. Explain why unbundling an insurance policy package is economically attractive to an insured. (p. 12.22)

4-2. List the incidental services customarily provided by insurers that an insurance buyer may choose to eliminate through unbundling. (p. 12.22)

4-3. Identify methods of compensation, in addition to determining payment through negotiation, that may be used for a contract claim administrator. (p. 12.23)

4-4. Identify risk financing program management questions with which an independent financial management service might assist in the risk finance planning process. (pp. 12.24–12.25)

Application Question

4-5. Unable to find an agent or broker familiar with the unique loss exposures of the aviation industry, XYZ Aviation's risk management professional decides to place different coverages through different agents and brokers. The risk management professional hires a different marketing intermediary for XYZ's general aviation liability, workers' compensation, and employee benefits. What are the potential problems that may develop as a result?

Educational Objective 5

Explain how to evaluate proposal responses, including:

- Services offered
- Financial stability of insurers
- Costs

Review Questions

5-1. List three criteria a risk management professional uses to evaluate risk financing services proposals. (p. 12.26)

5-2. Describe how a risk management professional uses the following three factors to evaluate coverage and service proposals: (pp. 12.27–12.28)

   a. Services offered

   b. Financial stability of insurers

   c. Costs

5-3. Identify objective factors a risk management professional may use to evaluate costs on retrospective rating insurance coverage proposals. (p. 12.28)

Application Question

5-4. Gallon Fluid Inc.'s insurance broker recommends that it obtain environmental pollution coverage with a nonstandard carrier. The insurer has a strong financial rating. However, Gallon's risk management professional wants to investigate potential associated risks with placing such important coverage with an unfamiliar insurer. Why should the risk management professional be concerned about a nonstandard insurer and what qualitative factors may the risk management professional consider?

Educational Objective 6
Describe the legal principles of insurance contracts.

Key Words and Phrases
Utmost good faith (p. 12.29)

Principle of disclosure (p. 12.29)

Representation (p. 12.30)

Misrepresentation (p. 12.30)

Concealment (p. 12.30)

Warranty (p. 12.30)

Affirmative warranty (p. 12.31)

Promissory warranty (p. 12.31)

Principle of equity (p. 12.31)

Estoppel (p. 12.32)

Contract of adhesion (p. 12.32)

Reasonable expectations (p. 12.33)

Parol evidence rule (p. 12.33)

Conditional contract (p. 12.34)

Principle of indemnity (p. 12.34)

Insurable interest (p. 12.35)

Subrogation (p. 12.37)

Review Questions

6-1. Describe three legal principles developed to handle the special problems associated with insurance. (pp. 12.29, 12.31, 12.33–12.34)

6-2. Explain possible insurance coverage implications of the following actions of an insured: (p. 12.30)
   a. Misrepresentation

b. Concealment

6-3. Identify occurrences in which a court is likely to rule that insurance remains in effect despite a breached condition. (p. 12.32)

6-4. Identify functions of an insurance contract that uphold the principle of indemnity. (p. 12.34)

Application Question

6-5. Sisterdale Corporation enters a sales contract to purchase an apartment complex. The closing on the property and transfer of the title to the property are not scheduled to occur until ninety days from the date of the sales contract. The sales contract specifies that the risk of loss remains with the seller of the property until closing. Sisterdale contacts its broker and requests that she obtain property insurance on the apartment complex immediately after the sales contract is signed. A fire destroys the apartment complex sixty days after the sales contract is signed and thirty days before the scheduled closing on the property. Who has an insurable interest in the property at the time of the fire?

Answers to Assignment 12 Questions

NOTE: These answers are provided to give students a basic understanding of acceptable types of responses. They often are not the only valid answers and are not intended to provide an exhaustive response to the questions.

Educational Objective 1

1-1. The following six steps are commonly involved in purchasing risk financing services:

   (1) The organization determines its insurance needs and develops specifications for coverage.

   (2) The organization presents its proposal to insurers through intermediaries.

   (3) Insurers and their intermediaries develop and present coverage proposals to the organization.

   (4) The organization evaluates the coverage proposals.

   (5) The organization enters into a contract with the insurer.

   (6) The organization implements steps related to the new coverage.

1-2. To determine specifications for exposures that will not be retained by the organization or transferred to a noninsurance transferee, a risk management professional assesses the organization's loss exposures, evaluates risk financing alternatives for dealing with potential losses from each, specifies the types and potential amounts of possible accidental losses that will not be retained or transferred, then develops insurance specifications for those exposures.

1-3. The authority to accept an insurer's coverage proposal depends on the proposal's wording, the insured organization's operating procedures, customary business practices between an insurer and its insured, and the written or oral process for communicating acceptance.

1-4. Depending on the insurer's marketing channels, Tarnely must hire an intermediary such as a broker, an independent agent, an exclusive agent, or, depending on the insurer's marketing channel, not hire an intermediary and contact the insurer directly. Care should also be taken to make each presentation to an insurer uniform, clear and complete. Meeting with each insurer is also helpful. To avoid potential difficulties when more than one intermediary represents the same insurer, it should be determined which intermediary will approach which insurer. Also, the presentations must reflect the current condition of Millwright. For example, if Millwright were to acquire a subsidiary, its coverage needs would obviously change.

Educational Objective 2

2-1. A risk management professional should consider the following marketing issues when placing or renewing insurance:

   - Nature of insurance marketing—The initiative for commercial insurance transactions can come from organizations seeking protection or from insurers seeking to gain more investable funds.

   - Market timing considerations—The frequency and scheduling of marketing efforts varies and should be performed only when a benefit greater than the cost can be expected.

   - Insurance specifications—Includes the underwriting information needed to comprehensively evaluate the risks an organization wishes to insure.

   - Competitive bidding—Bids are sought to obtain insurance through competitive bidding or a specified bidding process.

2-2. The following marketing activities should be performed by a risk management professional:
- Play an active role in seeking needed coverage.
- Establish criteria for selecting insurers, insurance marketing intermediaries, intermediaries' account executives, and providers of other risk management services.
- Assess the organization's loss exposures and identify which insurance contracts can best cover those exposures.
- Assist with making oral or written presentations to selected underwriters.
- Negotiate the final terms and the premium rates of each insurance contract the organization purchases.

2-3. An organization may obtain insurance using the following two categories of bidding:
   a. Open bidding—The organization places advertisements in insurance-related media or publications requesting bids from all intermediaries who meet certain qualifications.
   b. Closed, or selective, bidding—The organization invites only specific intermediaries who meet certain qualifications to submit bids.

2-4. The management at Gallon may prefer selective bidding of insurance accounts rather than open bidding at the renewal because it is comfortable with the rates and services that Danford has provided over the years.

Educational Objective 3

3-1. An organization may use the following four primary types of intermediaries to obtain insurance coverage:
   (1) Broker
   (2) Agent
   (3) Direct writing insurer
   (4) Risk management consultant

3-2. A risk management consultant is commonly hired to perform the following activities:
- Study an organization's loss exposures and recommend an appropriate risk management program
- Draft specifications for bidding an insurance program and analyze proposals
- Review the insurance coverages included in an organization's risk management program and compare them to those generally available in the current insurance market
- Audit an organization's risk management activities
- Conduct a feasibility study of proposals for establishing a captive insurance affiliate or a pool
- Draft a risk management procedures manual
- Design or conduct employee safety training programs
- Confirm the recommendations of an organization's own risk management professional

3-3. The following characteristics are necessary for the broker, agent, direct writing insurer, or risk management consultant:
- Technical expertise
- Financial resources

- Creativity
- Agreement on claim settlement approach
- Integrity

3-4. The following methods are used to compensate intermediaries:

   a. Sliding scale commission—Commission rates decrease for policies with large premiums, thus generating lower total commissions; used most frequently with workers' compensation insurance.

   b. Management fee—Compensation in which the intermediary waives the normal percentage commission and negotiates a minimum annual fee with each client.

3-5. A fee-for-service compensation could minimize a conflict of interest the broker may experience if a sound risk management recommendation were to reduce his commission income. Also, the broker's compensation may be less likely to be out of proportion to the effort expended on Parne's account, as may occur with traditional percentage commission.

Educational Objective 4

4-1. Unbundling an insurance policy package is economically attractive to the insured because the organization can conserve capital by removing incidental services such as claim administration and risk control services from its insurance coverage.

4-2. Incidental services customarily provided by insurers that an insurance buyer may choose to eliminate through unbundling include the following:
- Claim administration services
- Risk control services
- Risk management information services
- Financial management services
- Multiple intermediary marketing services
- Actuarial services

4-3. Methods of compensation, in addition to determining payment through negotiation, that may be used to pay a contract claim-handling administrator include the following:
- Percentage of settlement value
- Annual retainer—an amount subject to annual change that reflects the expected volume of work regardless of the value of the claims handled during the contract period
- Per-claim basis—an amount that varies by type of claim and by the number and types of claims likely to be litigated

4-4. Questions with which an independent financial management service may assist during the risk finance planning process include the following:
- How many and which loss exposures should be retained?
- What are the appropriate policy limits and deductibles for primary and excess insurance?
- In what financial instruments can any funded loss reserves be invested?
- How can an organization's captive insurance subsidiary be managed?

4-5. The risk management professional for XYZ may find that it will be more difficult to avoid gaps and overlaps when coordinating coverages. Another problem may develop regarding disputes about which insurer covers which loss. This will require the risk management professional to take a leadership role to provide communication and coordination among the insurers.

Educational Objective 5

5-1. Three criteria a risk management professional uses to evaluate risk financing services proposals are the following:
   (1) Services offered
   (2) Financial stability of insurers
   (3) Costs

5-2. A risk management professional uses the following three criteria to evaluate coverage and service proposals:
   (1) Services offered—Insure that each proposal received includes the same requested incidental services and that the services are of equal quality.
   (2) Financial stability of insurers—Evaluate qualitative factors in addition to overall financial ratings provided by industry-respected rating services.
   (3) Costs—Compare the costs of the proposed responses that have met the services offered criterion.

5-3. A risk management professional may use the following objective factors to evaluate costs on a retrospective rating coverage proposal:
   - Basic premium
   - Loss conversion factor (LCF)
   - Maximum chargeable losses
   - Maximum possible total cost

5-4. A nonstandard insurer's policies are not guaranteed by the state's guarantee fund in the event of the insurer's insolvency. Other qualitative factors Gallon's risk management professional may consider are the insurer's insurance product and geographic diversification, competitive position in the market, exposure to volatile lines of insurance, identity of any parent insurance company, adequacy of reserves, and stability of financial performance.

Educational Objective 6

6-1. The following three legal principles were developed to handle the special problems associated with insurance:
   (1) Disclosure—Every insurance applicant has a duty to disclose to the insurer and its legal agents all material information that could reasonably affect the insurer's underwriting decisions.
   (2) Equity—Requires the parties to an insurance contract to deal fairly with one another.
   (3) Indemnity—An insured's proceeds should not exceed its financial losses from an insured event.

6-2. Possible insurance coverage implications of the following actions of an insured include:
   a. Misrepresentation—The insurer may deny coverage for an insurance claim at the time of a loss if it can demonstrate to a court that the insured made a statement that is incorrect and material.

    b. Concealment—The insurer may refuse to pay for the loss and claim that had it known the information the insured concealed, it would have changed its underwriting of the policy.

6-3. A court is likely to rule that insurance remains in effect despite a breached condition when any of the following occur:
- The policy language expressing the condition was highly ambiguous.
- The insurer's representative, who allegedly waived the condition, had actual or apparent authority to do so.
- The actions of the insurer's representative were clearly intended to be a waiver or could reasonably have been interpreted to be a waiver.
- The additional hazard created by the breach was slight.

6-4. The following functions of insurance uphold the principle of indemnity:
- To pay for actual loss
- To require an insurable interest
- To prevent duplicate coverage
- To allow subrogation

6-5. An insurable interest in the apartment complex need not have existed when the property policy was obtained by Sisterdale's broker because Sisterdale, as the buyer of the property, did not have title yet but would have soon based on the terms of the sales contract. Sisterdale wanted to be sure coverage would have been in effect the moment it had ownership and, consequently, an insurable interest in the property. Since the fire destroyed the property before title transferred and before ownership of the property transferred to Sisterdale, the seller is the only party that had an insurable interest.

Direct Your Learning

Allocating Risk Management Costs

Educational Objectives

After learning the content of this assignment, you should be able to:

1. Describe the purposes of allocating risk management costs.

2. Describe the types of risk management costs an organization may want to allocate.

3. Describe the prospective and retrospective approaches to allocating risk management costs.

4. Describe the exposure bases and experience bases used to allocate risk management costs.

5. Describe the practical considerations of selecting an allocation basis.

6. Given a case, justify how risk management costs may be allocated among an organization's departments.

7. Define or describe each of the Key Words and Phrases for this assignment.

Study Materials

Required Reading:
- Risk Financing
  - Chapter 13

Study Aids:
- SMART Online Practice Exam
- SMART Study Aids
  - Review Notes and Flash Cards—Assignment 13

Outline

- **Purposes of a Risk Management Cost Allocation System**
  - A. Promote Risk Control
  - B. Facilitate Risk Retention
  - C. Prioritize Risk Management Expenditures
  - D. Reduce Costs
  - E. Distribute Costs Fairly
  - F. Balance Risk-Bearing and Risk-Sharing
  - G. Provide Managers With Risk Management Cost Information
- **Types of Risk Management Costs to Be Allocated**
  - A. Costs of Accidental Losses Not Reimbursed by Insurance or Other Outside Sources
  - B. Insurance Premiums
  - C. Costs of Risk Control Techniques
  - D. Costs of Administering Risk Management Activities
- **Approaches to Risk Management Cost Allocation**
  - A. Prospective Cost Allocation Approach
  - B. Retrospective Cost Allocation Approach
- **Bases for Risk Management Cost Allocation**
  - A. Exposure Bases
    1. General Liability
    2. Automobile Liability
    3. Workers' Compensation
    4. Property
    5. Other Exposures
  - B. Experience Basis
    1. Per Occurrence Limit
    2. Aggregate Limit
    3. Experience Period
  - C. Practical Considerations When Selecting an Allocation Basis
- **Case Study in Risk Management Cost Allocation**
- **Summary**

 When reviewing for your exam, remember to allot time for frequent breaks.

For each assignment, you should define or describe each of the Key Words and Phrases and answer each of the Review and Application Questions.

> ## Educational Objective 1
> Describe the purposes of allocating risk management costs.

Key Words and Phrases

Risk-bearing system (p. 13.5)

Risk-sharing system (p. 13.5)

Review Questions

1-1. On which costs of risk should a risk management cost allocation program focus? (p. 13.3)

1-2. Describe the purposes of an effective risk management cost allocation system. (pp. 13.3–13.7)

1-3. Describe how an organization may avoid internal and external manipulation of cost information provided by a risk management cost allocation system. (pp. 13.6–13.7)

Application Question

1-4. Foreway Corporation's marketing department has two divisions, one for its inside sales staff and one for its outside sales staff, which calls on customers in person. Each division has its own manager. The manager of the inside sales staff objects to the organization's allocation of the corporation's workers' compensation premium, which is currently split evenly among the two divisions. Foreway has 40 percent more employees involved in inside sales than in outside sales. However, the outside sales staff experiences workers' compensation losses that are ten times as frequent and severe as the inside staff's. Despite this, the manager of the outside sales division believes more of the workers' compensation premium should be allocated to the inside sales division because it employs more workers and consumes more payroll. How should Foreway's risk management professional resolve this dispute?

Educational Objective 2

Describe the types of risk management costs an organization may want to allocate.

Key Words and Phrases

Incurred loss basis (for allocating costs) (p. 13.8)

Claims-made basis (for allocating costs) (p. 13.8)

Claims-paid basis (for allocating costs) (p. 13.8)

Incurred but unpaid liabilities (p. 13.9)

Review Questions

2-1. Identify four types of risk management costs that can be fully or partially allocated that constitute an organization's cost of risk. (p. 13.7)

2-2. Identify the costs that are most appropriately allocated to a particular department within a company. (p. 13.7)

2-3. Describe the bases upon which an organization calculates loss costs. (p. 13.8)

2-4. Identify the costs associated with administering risk management activities. (p. 13.9)

Application Question

2-5. Galston's risk management professional believes her estimation of the organization's future retained losses may differ substantially from the actual losses it will incur over the next accounting period. If her estimate is too high, any excess funds allocated to and charged to a department can be returned. However, if her estimate is too low, Galston's financial health could be jeopardized if it does not have the resources it needs to pay the higher-than-expected retained losses. What can she do to prepare Galston for potential adverse fluctuations in its retained losses, and how should it account for the solution on its financial statements?

Educational Objective 3
Describe the prospective and retrospective approaches to allocating risk management costs.

Key Words and Phrases

Prospective cost allocation (p. 13.10)

Retrospective cost allocation (p. 13.10)

Review Questions

3-1. Describe the following widely used approaches to risk management cost allocation. (pp. 13.10–13.11)

   a. Prospective cost allocation

   b. Retrospective cost allocation

3-2. Describe the budgeting advantages of each of the following approaches to risk management cost allocation: (pp. 13.10–13.11)

   a. Prospective cost allocation

   b. Retrospective cost allocation

3-3. Describe how the ease of evaluating risk control program effectiveness differs depending on the cost allocation approach used. (pp. 13.10–13.11)

Application Question

3-4. XYZ Corporation's loss history has consistently been better than the industry average for the last five years. Management feels the risk control efforts of its departmental managers have, with few exceptions, been adequate. Senior management knows the corporation's board of directors believes that stable budgets indicate competent management. As the risk management professional for XYZ, would you recommend a prospective or retrospective cost allocation approach, and why?

Educational Objective 4

Describe the exposure bases and experience bases used to allocate risk management costs.

Key Words and Phrases

Exposure-based system (p. 13.11)

Experience-based system (p. 13.11)

Experience period (p. 13.17)

Review Questions

4-1. List characteristics used to measure a loss exposure for cost allocation purposes. (pp. 13.12–13.13)

4-2. Identify commonly used bases for measuring and allocating costs for the following loss exposures: (pp. 13.13–13.14)

   a. General liability

   b. Automobile liability

   c. Workers' compensation

   d. Property

4-3. Identify methods an organization might use to allocate risk management overhead. (p. 13.15)

4-4. List three primary criteria used to project a department's future losses and related costs. (p. 13.16)

Application Question

4-5. XYZ Corporation's risk management professional has learned the production department is about to launch a new product line. Several of the new products are being rushed to market due to intense competition and were not as thoroughly tested for safety as the risk management professional would have preferred. The corporation uses a prospective experience basis to allocate risk management costs. Explain what experience period the production department managers will likely request and, if granted, what tools the risk management professional can use to make the allocation equitable among the corporation's other departments in light of the high potential for future product liability claims.

Educational Objective 5
Describe the practical considerations of selecting an allocation basis.

Review Questions

5-1. List issues relevant to an organization when selecting a cost allocation system. (pp. 13.17–13.19)

5-2. Explain why some organizations may charge each department a minimum amount or maximum amount for risk management services. (p. 13.18)

5-3. Identify situations that typically trigger cost allocation system changes. (p. 13.19)

Application Question

5-4. Zelles is an international conglomerate with subsidiaries in several different countries. The management of each foreign subsidiary has been granted the authority to purchase its own insurance rather than participate in a centralized risk management cost allocation system. What problems may this create for a risk management professional responsible for appropriate cost allocation for the entire conglomerate?

Educational Objective 6

Given a case, justify how risk management costs may be allocated among an organization's departments.

Application Question

6-1. Ace Manufacturing Company's risk management professional wishes to allocate the organization's upcoming $180,000 annual products liability premium among Departments A, B, and C, the departments that produce the organization's three products. The allocations are to be based one-third on each department's sales for the past year and two-thirds on the products liability claims paid for each department's products over the past three years, with the portion of each claim charged to each department capped at $25,000. The relevant sales and capped paid claim dollar amounts are as follows:

	1	2	3	4	5	6
Department	Sales (millions)	Percentage of total sales: $\dfrac{\text{Sales per department}}{\text{Total}}$	Losses (thousands)	Percentage of total losses: $\dfrac{\text{Losses per department}}{\text{Total}}$	Weighted percentage (1/3 sales and 2/3 losses): $\dfrac{[\text{Col. 2} + (2 \times \text{Col. 4})]}{3}$	Allocation per department of the $180,000 products liability premium: $\left(\dfrac{\text{Col. 5}}{100}\right) \times \$180{,}000$
A	80		30			
B	40		20			
C	20		60			
Total	$140	100	$110	100	100	$180,000

By entering the missing values in the table above, calculate each department's premium allocation for products liability insurance for the coming year.

Answers to Assignment 13 Questions

NOTE: These answers are provided to give students a basic understanding of acceptable types of responses. They often are not the only valid answers and are not intended to provide an exhaustive response to the questions.

Educational Objective 1

1-1. An effectively designed risk management cost allocation system should focus on the following costs of risk:
- Retained losses
- Insurance premiums
- Risk control costs
- Administrative expenses for the risk management function.

1-2. An effective cost allocation system serves the following purposes:
- Promote risk control—Motivates personnel to reduce the frequency and/or severity of the organization's losses because each department is held accountable or rewarded for its risk control efforts.
- Facilitate risk retention—Allows the entire organization to benefit from an optimal risk retention level, while not unduly exposing individual departments to excessive fluctuations in their cost of risk.
- Prioritize risk management expenditures—Departments that pay for risk control measures carefully scrutinize the measure's cost effectiveness and prioritize measures that provide the greatest return on investment.
- Reduce costs—Lowering claim frequency and severity through risk control allows an organization to retain risk at an optimal level, resulting in a lower cost of risk.
- Distribute costs fairly—Allocated amounts should have a direct correlation between departmental losses and the amount of risk management costs allocated to the unit.
- Balance risk-bearing and risk-sharing—A proper balance distributes risk management costs across the organization while also allowing departments to benefit from their own loss experience and other changing conditions.
- Provide managers with risk management cost information—Accurate allocation and reporting of cost of risk compels managers to focus on areas in which the cost of risk can be reduced.

1-3.
- Internal manipulation of cost information can be discouraged or prevented by requiring losses to be reviewed or audited to confirm that they were reported in a timely fashion and that subsequent changes to reserve amounts are not attributable to facts that should have been revealed at the time of the loss.
- External manipulation may be prevented if the system is designed to reflect the organization's overall objectives and has been approved by senior management.

1-4. An effective cost allocation system addresses the concerns of both division managers. The inside sales division appears to have more exposure at first glance because of its higher number of employees and its larger payroll. However, the outside sales division has far more frequent and severe claims than the inside sales division. Some risk management professionals would argue that this is because outside sales jobs are much riskier. Consequently, the outside sales division's overall workers' compensation loss exposure is higher than the inside sales division's. Therefore, the most equitable solution is to increase the outside sales division's premium allocation. The manager of the inside sales division should be satisfied with the decreased premium allocation. The manager of the outside sales division should focus on preventing or reducing the frequency and severity of the division's losses.

Educational Objective 2

2-1. Four types of risk management costs that constitute an organization's cost of risk are as follows:
 (1) Costs of accidental losses not reimbursed by insurance or other outside sources
 (2) Insurance premiums
 (3) Costs of risk control techniques
 (4) Costs of administering risk management activities

2-2. Costs most appropriately allocated to a department include those that are clearly incurred by or beneficial to the department and that are wholly within its control.

2-3. An organization calculates loss costs based on one the following:
 - Incurred loss basis—Amount is paid for losses are added to reserves for pending claims, to the additions to those reserves, and to the estimated amount of incurred but not reported losses.
 - Claims-made basis—Actual loss payments are added to changes in reserves for claims made during the accounting period.
 - Claims-paid basis—Amount paid on losses during the accounting period, regardless of when the losses wee incurred.

2-4. Costs associated with administering risk management activities include the following:
 - Operating budget of the risk management department
 - Cost of executives' time from other departments
 - Other resources from other departments devoted to risk management

2-5. The risk management professional should consider adding a risk charge when calculating retained losses that are to be allocated. The risk charge is an amount added to an organization's expected losses to cover potential adverse fluctuation in experience. The risk charge is not a liability and should not be shown as such on Galston's financial statements. It should be shown as a segregated part of Galston's equity.

Educational Objective 3

3-1. Two general approaches to risk management cost allocation are as follows:
 a. Prospective cost allocation system—Estimated costs are allocated at the beginning of the accounting period during which they are expected to be incurred, but once allocated, costs are not changed for the period.
 b. Retrospective cost allocation system—Estimated costs are allocated at the beginning of the accounting period during which they are expected to be incurred, but can be reallocated one or more times during or after the close of the period.

3-2. The following are the advantages of the given risk management cost allocation approaches:
   a. Prospective cost allocation approach—Costs are assumed to be known before the beginning of the accounting period and are not changed.
   b. Retrospective approach—Costs are more accurately attributed to the period and department with which they are associated. However, final allocated costs are not determined until well after the end of the period during which the losses were incurred, which complicates risk management budgeting.

3-3. The ease of evaluating the effectiveness of a risk control program differs as follows, depending on the cost allocation approach:
   - Prospective cost allocation—An increase (or decrease) in risk control activity can be separated by several accounting periods from the corresponding reduction (or increase) in allocated costs and are not always reflective of risk control expense outputs of the period to which they are charged.
   - Retrospective cost allocation—Risk control program effectiveness is facilitated because the decrease (or increase) in loss costs is immediately recognized in terms of allocated costs.
   - XYZ should adopt a prospective cost allocation approach because such an approach typically produces a more stable budget, which is important to the Board of Directors. XYZ's losses have also been stable and below the industry average, which indicates its departmental managers are practicing appropriate risk control. This also suggests that prospective cost allocation would be the best approach.

Educational Objective 4

4-1. Characteristics used to measure a loss exposure for cost allocation purposes include size, nature of operations, and territory.

4-2. Commonly used bases for measuring and allocating costs for loss exposures include the following:
   a. General liability—Square footage of floor space, annual budget, payroll, full-time-equivalent workers, and sales.
   b. Automobile liability—Number of vehicles used, with some adjustments for differences in types of vehicles.
   c. Workers' compensation—Payroll and full-time equivalent number of employees, with adjustments made for differences in exposure by job classification.
   d. Property—Square footage and property values (either replacement cost or actual cash value). The exposure base is often modified to accurately reflect the associated exposure.

4-3. An organization may use the following methods to allocate risk management overhead:
   - In proportion to the total of other risk management department costs allocated for particular exposures
   - As a fixed percentage of some other bases, such as sales
   - As a combination of a flat fee per department (to cover fixed costs) and a percentage of some base, such as sales (to cover variable costs)

4-4. The three primary criteria used to project a department's losses and related costs are the following:
   1. Changes in claims paid

2. Changes in payments plus loss reserves
3. Changes in projected ultimate incurred losses

4-5. XYZ's production department managers are likely to favor an extended reporting period (for example, a full five years). A longer experience period should make the cost allocation formula less responsive to changes in recent past loss experience, which limits the fluctuation of charges that results from unusually bad claim experience. In response, the risk management professional can weight the multiyear experience period to more heavily count recent experience. For example, if the production managers are granted a five-year experience period, the most recent year can be weighted by 20 percent, the second and third years weighted by 15 percent each, and the fourth and fifth years weighted by 10 percent each.

Educational Objective 5

5-1. Issues relevant when selecting a cost allocation system include the following:
- Accounting system
- Tax system
- Minimum and maximum risk management costs to be charged to departments
- Whether insurance is purchased by individual departments
- Amount of risk management cost relative to a department's total budget
- How the department's risk management costs results correlate to that manager's bonus and budget
- Senior management's support of the cost allocation system
- The RMIS used
- Consistency of cost allocation

5-2. Some organizations may charge each department a minimum amount for risk management services to incorporate an exposure basis within the risk management cost allocation system. A maximum amount might be charged to reduce the fluctuations in allocated costs from one accounting period to the next.

5-3. The following situations typically trigger cost allocation system changes:
- Material shifts in the organization's operations
- Change in expected losses due to change in legal climate, inflation, or some other factor, which can create a need to change the per occurrence limit
- Restructuring the organization's departments or lines of authority

5-4 When each subsidiary purchases its own insurance, the combined purchasing power of the organization as a whole is not leveraged. This limits the subsidiaries' ability to negotiate lower expense factors and service fees from an insurer. Also, gaps in coverage or duplications of coverage may result. In addition, consistent application of umbrella or excess liability insurance policies presents a challenge.

Educational Objective 6

6-1. The allocations for Departments A, B, and C (the values in Column 6) are calculated as follows:

	1	2	3	4	5	6
Department	Sales (millions)	Percentage of total sales: $\dfrac{\text{Sales per department}}{\text{Total}}$	Losses (thousands)	Percentage of total losses: $\dfrac{\text{Losses per department}}{\text{Total}}$	Weighted percentage (1/3 sales and 2/3 losses): $\dfrac{[\text{Col. 2} + (2 \times \text{Col. 4})]}{3}$	Allocation per department of the $180,000 products liability premium: $\left(\dfrac{\text{Col. 5}}{100}\right) \times \$180{,}000$
A	80	57	30	27	37	66,600
B	40	29	20	18	22	39,600
C	20	14	60	55	41	73,800
Total	140	100	110	100	100	180,000

Exam Information

About Institute Exams

Exam questions are based on the Educational Objectives stated in the course guide and textbook. The exam is designed to measure whether you have met those Educational Objectives. The exam does not test every Educational Objective. Instead, it tests over a balanced sample of Educational Objectives.

How to Prepare for Institute Exams

What can you do to prepare for an Institute exam? Students who pass Institute exams do the following:

- Use the assigned study materials. Focus your study on the Educational Objectives presented at the beginning of each course guide assignment. Thoroughly read the textbook and any other assigned materials, and then complete the course guide exercises. Choose a study method that best suits your needs; for example, participate in a traditional class, online class, or informal study group; or study on your own. Use the Institutes' SMART Study Aids (if available) for practice and review. If this course has an associated SMART Online Practice Exams product, you will find an access code on the inside back cover of this course guide. This access code allows you to print (in PDF format) a full practice exam and to take additional online practice exams that will simulate an actual credentialing exam.

- Become familiar with the types of test questions asked on the exam. The practice exam in this course guide or in the SMART Online Practice Exams product will help you understand the different types of questions you will encounter on the exam.

- Maximize your test-taking time. Successful students use the sample exam in the course guide or in the SMART Online Practice Exams product to practice pacing themselves. Learning how to manage your time during the exam ensures that you will complete all of the test questions in the time allotted.

Types of Exam Questions

The exam for this course consists of objective questions of several types.

The Correct-Answer Type

In this type of question, the question stem is followed by four responses, one of which is absolutely correct. Select the *correct* answer.

> Which one of the following persons evaluates requests for insurance to determine which applicants are accepted and which are rejected?
>
> a. The premium auditor
>
> b. The loss control representative
>
> c. The underwriter
>
> d. The risk manager

The Best-Answer Type

In this type of question, the question stem is followed by four responses, only one of which is best, given the statement made or facts provided in the stem. Select the *best* answer.

> Several people within an insurer might be involved in determining whether an applicant for insurance is accepted. Which one of the following positions is primarily responsible for determining whether an applicant for insurance is accepted?
>
> a. The loss control representative
>
> b. The customer service representative
>
> c. The underwriter
>
> d. The premium auditor

The Incomplete-Statement or Sentence-Completion Type

In this type of question, the last part of the question stem consists of a portion of a statement rather than a direct question. Select the phrase that *correctly* or *best* completes the sentence.

Residual market plans designed for individuals who are unable to obtain insurance on their personal property in the voluntary market are called

a. VIN plans.

b. Self-insured retention plans.

c. Premium discount plans.

d. FAIR plans.

"All of the Above" Type

In this type of question, only one of the first three answers could be correct, or all three might be correct, in which case the best answer would be "All of the above." Read all the answers and select the *best* answer.

When a large commercial insured's policy is up for renewal, who is likely to provide input to the renewal decision process?

a. The underwriter

b. The loss control representative

c. The producer

d. All of the above

"All of the following, EXCEPT:" Type

In this type of question, responses include three correct answers and one answer that is incorrect or is clearly the least correct. Select the *incorrect* or *least correct* answer.

All of the following adjust insurance claims, EXCEPT:

a. Insurer claim representatives

b. Premium auditors

c. Producers

d. Independent adjusters